Losing It

Also by Lara Harte
First Time

Losing It

LARA HARTE

PHOENIX HOUSE
London

First published in Great Britain
in 1999 by Phoenix House

A CIP catalogue record for this book
is available from the British Library.

ISBN 1 861591 37 3 (cased)
1 861591 52 7 (trade paperback)

Typeset by Deltatype Ltd, Birkenhead, Merseyside
Printed in Great Britain by
Clays Ltd, St Ives plc

Phoenix House
An imprint of the Weidenfeld & Nicolson Division of
The Orion Publishing Group Ltd
Orion House
5 Upper Saint Martin's Lane
London, WC2H 9EA

One

The air smokes: my cigarette, my state of mind. I light another, feeding the atmosphere. Corinne fans it away, her silver rings glint like conquering steel – she's given up smoking. I'm burning away. She's my sister, I need her now.

Corinne came home, for a week, maybe two. I miss her when she's in England. She hates Dublin. Mam's been fussing over her from the minute she walked in the door – she's spent the last week cleaning up the house, and she's even done the living room up so now there's white wallpaper with big blue flowers instead of white wallpaper with little pink flowers.

Corinne sits at her bedroom window, staring at the little houses on the other side of the road that match the ones on our side and the houses on the road beyond that and the road beyond that again. It doesn't feel like her room anymore. More like a spare room, with nothing but new flowery wallpaper and empty white furniture and the shitty little ornaments Mam buys in pound shops and litters the house with to make it look nice – dogs, cats, milkmaids and flower-baskets. Still, as long as they're not brown or yellow, I can restrain myself from smashing them to pieces.

I watch her from the bed. She puts her feet up on the desk at the wall and tilts the chair back so it's supported by the opposite wall. She's wearing a bright blue top; it suits her, with the long dark hair and big blue eyes. It'd look stupid on me though, and I look like her. Corinne and Merle Murphy – why Mam had to call us that, I will never understand.

'So it's all over now, band and everything,' I explained.

'Like I told you, you're better off that way. He's an asshole.'

I went out with Aidan for three whole years. Three years during which we had the best band around here. He sang with the most amazing voice I'd ever heard and I played guitar. But things changed, no matter how hard I tried to keep them the same. I'd hoped that we could really make something of ourselves, so I put all my effort into the band and got really good on the guitar. The others were pretty enthusiastic too, even if they weren't as intense about the whole thing as I was.

All enthusiastic, except for Aidan. It seemed that the better I got, the more it put him off. Oh he wanted to go places all right; more than that, he wanted to be the centre of attention, the most important person in the band. But you can't do that and be all that if you don't put the work in, and he became very lazy in the last year. Sometimes he'd turn up to band practice an hour late, sometimes he wouldn't come at all. Often he wouldn't know the songs, especially if I'd written them, and that hurt a lot. Eventually, he broke it off with me. I wasn't surprised, but I was still very upset. I tried to keep the band going anyway, because I believed in it so much. But I just found it too difficult to be around him – he was so nasty to me all the time now. So I decided to leave.

'That whole thing fucked up my head completely,' I told Corinne.

'Well that's understandable, you put a lot into it.'

She didn't know the half of it. I'd been waiting weeks to tell her, and now, finally, she was here.

'I hated myself,' I said. 'These past few months, I've hated myself for being in that band and not being able to do anything about the way things were going. So I'd come home from band practice and cut myself and that'd calm me down.'

She took her feet off the desk and turned to face me, gripping her knees with her hands. She had blue nail varnish on, stark against her skin.

'I didn't want to let him get to me, and I thought, if anyone's going to hurt me, it'll be me, I'm not going to cry over him, it won't be over him. And I was so angry as well, I just wanted to hurt someone, and I thought that if I hurt myself, I wouldn't need to hurt anybody else. And it worked. So then I pushed the idea further. We all get good times and bad times, and I told myself that if I got so much pain now, then I'd get less later on, because if life's what you make it yourself, then it's whatever you believe yourself that's true, and I believed this.'

Corinne didn't look shocked, she never was. She was just a bit surprised.

'So why are you so upset then, if it worked?' she asked quietly.

'It's fucking psycho stuff. Of course I'm worried, aren't you?'

'No, I don't think it's a problem, as long as you've got it worked out and can contain it. The way I see it, anyone that's completely different has their own way of looking at things, so if that's how you coped, then that's fine, because all you're doing is coping in your own way.'

She was so calm, didn't she care? She drove me mad just sitting there, with those eyes that always looked like they saw everything: magnets, sucking everything in, so steady.

'Well you wanted reassurance, didn't you?' she asked.

Yes, I thought, reassurance was what I'd asked for, but that's not what I wanted. I had expected her to tell me where I'd gone wrong, which was stupid of me, because then I'd feel worse, for not having seen that myself. I just wanted peace of mind. And she couldn't give that to me, so this conversation had achieved nothing. I think fundamentally I just needed to talk to her so that

I wouldn't feel isolated, but that wasn't an end in itself, and anyway, it hadn't worked.

'Don't you even care that my life's falling to pieces?' I asked, feeling panicked because this conversation had gone so wrong.

'No it isn't,' she answered. 'Like I said, you're better off, you'll find a new band soon.'

No, I won't. There's no one as good as we were anywhere around here. Oh I can look alright, I can look all over Dublin and eventually I'll find one. But I couldn't bring myself to do that just yet, it was too soon. I needed time to let the memories and the anger fade away into shadows.

'In fact,' said Corinne, 'you'll probably be able to find one in college.'

It was September, and I was supposed to be going to college this year. Oh God. I did not feel like discussing it now. It was late, and I had to meet my friend Hannah in a pub in town. I needed a drink. I was glad now that Corinne wasn't coming. She'd said she was tired, and couldn't face walking all the way down to the bus stop and having to wait hours for a bus. She hated being stuck in the middle of nowhere. If she wasn't so tired she'd come. She hated being cooped up in this house – all that flowery wallpaper. But Mam was thrilled to have her here. Corinne was bored out of her mind, but at least she didn't live here any more. I did.

I didn't have to get ready to go out, I was always done up. Once, when I was twelve and Corinne was sixteen, I had asked her why she always wore a ton of make-up. She laughed and told me that she used to wear it only when she was going out – a night out used to be a big deal to her and her friends. But then they started going out drinking so often that all the excitement went out of it. Corinne said that the thing about make-up was, if you thought you looked good, then you expected something to happen, so when it didn't, you were disappointed, because you had been expecting it. She said it was kind of stupid of her, really, but she started doing herself up all the time so that it wouldn't be special anymore.

I never thought of it that way; I always dressed the same. How did I dress? I don't know. Not like Corinne, she went to a lot of trouble to look exotic.

I sat on my bed for a while, staring at the walls, thinking about Corinne and all that tension, putting off going out as long as I could. I was calmer in here with my sea-green walls and purple velvet curtains diluting the colour of that awful carpet – it was a crappy insipid blue, just like the colour of the painted veil on a statue of the Virgin Mary. Ten years ago, my mother had bought enough of that carpet to cover the whole house because it was going cheap. Not my style though. I liked strong, deep, vibrant colours; black and white, like my guitar.

All good things come to an end though. I piled on the lipstick in the full-length mirror near the window. It was a plain mirror with no frame – I'd have liked a fancier one, but I couldn't afford it and I had better things to do with what little money came my way from the local bloody supermarket. Guitar and drink. I looked in the mirror again, maybe I should have got changed, I'm beginning to get bored with these black jeans and the top. Oh well, I can't be bothered, what does it matter, anyway?

I said goodbye to my mother. She was sitting in the kitchen drinking tea with one of the neighbours. How can that be enough for her? Mam means well, though. Our dad died when I was little, so she's all we've got.

It was sunny outside, but I had to go out early tonight because the place I was going to gets busy, and it was a Saturday night. I wanted a seat. So I was going to miss the sunset, one of those summer salmon-pink death-beds. Oh God, I'm going to have to stop associating things with pain. Whenever I look at the guitar these days, all I can think of is Aidan, and even though I've stopped cutting myself, I look at the guitar and remember how much my fingers hurt when I was learning to play, and how I was so anxious to learn as fast as I could that I'd keep practising until my fingers bled. I'd play on and on, waiting for the strained back and aching muscles, hanging on until the blood came. Eventually, the tips of my fingers grew hard and the blood stopped. Even so, I sometimes pushed myself to pain, but I was always on such a high by the time I got there that it became just another edge on the whole experience.

Guitar was heaven, and it was reality. It was all I needed. But I wanted it to go somewhere. I wanted my life to mean something more than a college degree. Everyone thought Corinne was great for having one, but my intelligent sister didn't even know what she wanted to do with her life. In fact, the only thing Corinne seemed to know was that she didn't want to be here, and that was scary.

Two

I met my friend Hannah in her favourite pub in town. She lives just across the road from me, but I'd arranged to meet her in here because she was already in town. Every week, she comes here to this pub and shines, and then she carries away the memories and impressions of the night with her, to keep her shining until the next night out. Last week, I was very depressed because I'd been thinking a lot about Aidan, so I came here with Hannah to get wasted enough to forget about him. It worked. But usually, I just sit back and soak up all the atmosphere.

Hannah's the nicest person in the world. Most of the time. She'd do anything for anyone. John was here with her tonight. She was wearing her new red dress and she had new blonde highlights in her long wavy hair. He seems a nice enough fella. She only met him last week and this is my first time to see him. He has a good personality, so he's good to have with you on a night out like this. He's not bad-looking either. And she says she likes him. Even though the most important thing for her about him is that he's in the same college we're meant to be going to – handy for her when the time comes.

Don't get the wrong idea about Hannah. I know her so well that, to me, her using John is just a detail, something to feel vaguely sorry for her about. You see, going to college is the most important thing in her life, and I don't mean that in an ordinary young-person sense. Hannah grew up drowning, in a family swamped in trauma while her brother Shane was around. After he left, her parents closed off into themselves and away from Hannah. He's a heroin-addict, left home when she was twelve. Otherwise he'd have been kicked out.

Nobody's seen or heard from him since. The family just doesn't want to know. You can't blame them, really. He robbed them blind. The day before he left for good, he came to the house around four in the morning. Didn't have a key, so he smashed the glass in the door. Her mam was terrified it would happen again, and that the place would be broken into again, but she wanted to keep glass in her door because she liked seeing the hall light shining through the glass when she got home after dark. So she got new glass and put bars behind all the doors and windows downstairs. Inside, they had the house done up lovely, but they were left with these hideous bars and an alienated Hannah, who had been severely affected by the whole business.

She was desperate not to become her brother. That was why college was so important, it would give her a positive life, outside all that. That was why we were sitting here with John. He turned to me, smiling.

'You're starting college too, aren't you?'

What was I to say? I could have been diplomatic, but I was still all wound up from Corinne.

'Well actually, no, I don't think so.' I looked at Hannah. This subject always aroused emotion – we'd been best friends for a long time, and she'd always planned that we'd go together, so that at least we'd have each other. Because what if it didn't work out? How were we to know what it was like? The only person we knew really well that had gone to college was Corinne, and even her reassurances weren't enough for Hannah.

'Don't mind her, of course she's going. She's got her place and everything. She even took a year off after school like me, so that she'd have some money saved.'

'So what's the story then? Do you not want to go anymore?' he asked.

'No.'

'Tell her she's being stupid,' Hannah told him. He looked a bit uncomfortable, he didn't want to get involved. On the other hand, I could see him thinking that he was there with her, and it was in his interest to please her.

'Well, like, you have to do something, you know,' he said. The way he said it annoyed me.

'Just because I don't do something your way doesn't mean I'm not doing anything,' I told him.

'Merle!' said Hannah. I'd gone and antagonized her, which was exactly what I'd told myself I wouldn't do.

'Don't mind me,' I appealed to him. 'It's just that it's a touchy subject, and my sister's home on holiday . . .'

'Oh right, do you not get on with her or something?' he asked.

'No, I do,' I said, surprised. 'That wasn't what I meant . . .'

Hannah filled in the silence for me. 'Corinne must have told you to go to college then, did she? That's what you mean.'

I didn't tell her we hadn't talked about it, I didn't say anything, just twirled the pint glass in my hand, watched the brown storm wave swirling, thinking how being with Hannah always used to calm me down.

She turned to John. 'Corinne's just so cool. Merle's into music you see, she plays guitar and stuff. That's why she doesn't want to go to college. But I reckoned Corinne'd talk her around, because she used to be really into music, even though she never played anything, and Merle always looked up to her, and she told me last time she was over that Merle'd be stupid not to get some kind of qualification behind her as well . . .'

Storm wave swirling. I don't know what I'm going to do.

9

Control, I want control. I'm burning away. I've watched everyone I know choose one of the two options open to them: some are in college, some are on the dole. I could go either way. I'll go neither.

I just wanted to hold myself apart from everything, because that would keep me safe, but it was like stretching an elastic band: the tauter I got, the closer I felt to the point of disintegration.

Three

Seems like I needed something to happen. Something did. Two days later. Only it stayed outside me. I was emotionally untouched on Monday night when Mam rang Spar to say she was in the hospital with Corinne. My sister had swallowed a few bottles of pills and Mam had found her lying on her bedroom floor when she got home from work. As soon as Mam saw me, she collapsed, and I was plunged into a landscape of her shock, tears and self-blame.

Don't you love your sister, I ask myself with creeping revulsion. Because if I do, I can't feel it. I always assumed I must, but I can't feel it. I don't seem to care whether I ever see her again, whether she lives or dies. I don't care?

My mother's in pieces and she can't cope. Neither of us can believe it.

I feel completely detached from everything that's happening around me. All I can think is that this act gives her shape: she's confined now, closed at each end, she has a beginning and an end. I can be objective about her now, because I can see her as something tangible, manageable.

Corinne, Corinne, you will die perfectly, won't you? You've got control now, the ultimate control. You will always be a mystery. You will always compel us with fascination and fear. Like a dead star.

Why amn't I upset? I should be crying my eyes out, instead of seeing something strange and beautiful from a distance, instead of fixing my sister in my head as a cult image. I should be cursing myself for not having seen any signs, for putting pressure on her with my problems . . . But remember what she said, she said that if I could find a way of coping with my own problems, no matter what it was, then that was fine. That's all she's doing, isn't it? She's just escaping from something she wants to leave behind.

You bitch, I tell myself, you should be horrified by the lengths she's gone to. You should be wracked with anguish and guilt . . . And I am, I am tearing myself to pieces because I'm not upset over Corinne.

Corinne lived to haunt me. I had hoped that when I saw her again I'd unfreeze, that seeing her would spark up a reaction and I'd at least feel something like relief that she was OK. But seeing her only consolidated my state of mind. Poor girl, she felt so guilty for having hurt everyone so much, and she spent the first few days apologizing to and reassuring Mam.

Everyone seemed to understand why it had happened – those who knew about it, that is, the neighbours didn't know, not many people knew. She'd had a bad break-up with someone in England. Her friend Maeve flew over from England for the weekend to see her, and she told me and Mam all about it. Corinne really had gone all weird, she said, staying up all night every night in her room, drinking by herself.

Everyone wanted to help her. She got the works. Me and Mam sitting and smiling with her in case she needed to talk or not, whichever she preferred. Chocolate, drink, Mam bringing her to the beach for the day, videos, town, the pub. There was all that counselling shit as well.

I still couldn't bring myself to react emotionally to her, no matter how hard I tried. On the one hand, I was thinking, thank God, you've given us something interesting to think and talk about, as if she was nothing more than a bit of local scandal or something in the news. And on the other hand, I was thinking, oh my God, I'm trapped now, I have to go to college. Things were bad enough without laying all that worry on Mam as well. No. But no matter how much I hated myself for this coldness, I couldn't manage to bring what Corinne had done any closer to my feelings.

I tried to act normal around Corinne. She tried to act normal with me. It's not that there was a barrier between us. It was more like a relationship with someone you run into once in a while, someone you're friendly with but don't know very well. She said at an early stage that she didn't want to talk about what she had done any more, at least not with me. She didn't have to force herself with me, she said, she could just let the subject drop without feeling guilty. She could relax, be herself. And yet it was a very superficial interaction. We kept our deepest and darkest sides concealed from one another.

A Sunday morning came. The day before Corinne was to go away again with her restlessness. Mam said me and Corinne had to go to Mass with her. If we never went again, fair enough, she said, but she wanted us to go just this once. We could see how much it meant to her for us to go.

That Mass was the breakthrough between me and Corinne. Walking into the stifled darkness, we felt something stirring from childhood. So long since I'd been in a church. I hated churches. There was so little air inside them that I always felt as if I was about to be suffocated. Outside, weak rain would still be falling in a sky the colour of an ageing white veil. Inside, babies cried, kids got bored and messed, me and Corinne looked at each other and empathized.

Next to the church is the local. There's always something sinister about our local pub during the daytime. It has small windows that maintain the impression of darkness throughout the day. But daylight can still penetrate, weakening the effect of the artificial light, reducing the light bulbs to nothing more than small orange glows that cheapen the colours of the place, even though at night they brighten like fire.

Corinne had wanted to die because self-hatred was all she had inside. Her life meant nothing to her, she said. You see, she was unable to feel any real emotion about anything. For example, she said, she had been going out with someone, and she had liked the idea of this person so much that she had tried as hard as she could to feel something for him. But she remained emotionally untouched. No matter how hard she tried, she couldn't make him seem any more real to her than a dream.

We sat there all day, drinking pints of Bud that shone like fool's gold in an imitation heaven. I was relating so well to Corinne now that I could have cried at her obvious pain.

If only she had been able to make the connection with him, she said. But it was no use. It was as if there were mounds of dead stuff all around her, blocking her path. And no matter how hard she tried to care about him at the time, and no matter how hard she tried to convince herself afterwards that she might have felt something, there was nothing she could do to stem the tide of self-hatred, confusion, and despair. And so what she felt was the loaded intensity of an imminent, destructive storm. She allowed it to overwhelm her and tried to make it end her life, but she survived. I could see the sheen on her eyes. Glow of tears.

A large crowd came into the pub – a load of adults and their kids. The kids settled opposite us, with the crisps and Coke that always, always, I remembered, tasted stale in a pub. 'Do you remember that?' I asked her, but she was in another world and didn't hear me. It seemed to me that if I even got the faintest smell of the kids' Coke glasses, I'd get high on the deathly scent of stagnation.

14

There was no music today, just some important match on the radio. We'd deliberately chosen this pub to avoid the mind-numbing noise and distraction of a big-screen showing of whatever match it was.

'Anything you ever do,' said Corinne, 'any job you ever work at, any college you ever go to, any fella you ever go out with . . . it's, it's as if you're just acting out a passive role and things are happening along an empty, predetermined course. So that means that things happen to you just as they're supposed to and just as you think they're going to, only they don't seem to have anything to do with you, because they don't touch you and you can't feel them. They're just not real, you know? And then you panic, and you say, no! This job, this boyfriend, this life, it's not what I want. But you can't figure out what it is you want.'

She was panicking now, just thinking about it. I sat there in a state of confusion, blaming myself for never having seen that Corinne was such a mess. She drank some more while I waited for her to explain.

'And then,' she continued, 'you realize that the reason why you don't know what you want or what's wrong with you is because your feelings have been switched off somewhere along the way. You discover you haven't been using them. You've just been living out some kind of routine distanced from yourself and from the world because your emotions have moved so far away from you that you end up feeling nothing about anything or anyone.'

'Are you sure?' I asked her.

She didn't give me her answer, but I knew it anyway. This wasn't just the drink talking, she meant every word of it. Corinne was so sure of herself that she wasn't even questioning all this. She was just letting wave after wave of this stuff pull us both down deeper and deeper into some dark place. And even though part of me wanted to go with her, something was resisting. There must be a reason why she had become so frozen-up emotionally – even though I hadn't been able to find a reason for why I myself had frozen-up emotionally the night she tried to kill herself, no matter how hard I'd tried. But something in me was crying out for an explanation.

'If that's what made you want to kill yourself, why did you wait until you'd come back here?' I couldn't help myself, I had to ask her. She started to look upset for the first time all day, but it wasn't enough to stop me from tearing the next sentence out: 'I'm sorry, Corinne, but you must see that it would have been harder on Mam if you'd died under her roof – if it had been in England, then at least she could have been sure it was nothing to do with her.'

'Oh, would she not think that maybe I missed her and that that had something to do with me killing myself?'

She swallowed back on a hoarse voice, but I said nothing. Nothing, because Corinne had always made it so clear that she hated it here, had to get out of the country – she was even leaving tomorrow morning . . .

'No, you're right, I suppose,' said Corinne. 'I don't think I'd finally made up my mind to do it until the day I did it, and I did it in such a rush that I just didn't think about things like what would you and Mam think. Something set me off, freaked me out, on top of everything else . . . But I didn't want to tell you about it. Somehow, it wasn't the fact of seeing this person that threw me, it was what it stood for.'

'Who did you see?' I asked, hoping that this would explain everything.

'Shane,' she said quietly.

Shane. Hannah's brother? I stared at her: 'Jesus Christ, where did you see him? What happened?'

'Nothing, it just proves what I've been saying – about not having an emotional connection with things. I saw him on

16

Saturday night. Sinéad rang me – you know the Sinéad I was in college with? And I decided that I would go out after all. So I was waiting for her in this pub – it's a new pub, and, and . . . Anyway, I saw Shane while I was sitting there looking out for her, but I couldn't bring myself to go over to him – he left not long after I spotted him . . .'

'But what was the big deal about that, Corinne? It would have been a bit of a shock alright, seeing as no one's seen him in so long, but . . . Did he look like he was in a bad way or what?'

Corinne was almost in a trance, though. She was somewhere my words couldn't pierce through to.

'I told you – I'm sitting in this pub, completely surrounded by strangers, and my eye focuses on one of them, and I see it's Shane. But now he's a stranger, and I feel nothing, just completely distanced and passive, because I know that, sooner or later, one of us is going to leave, without ever having acknowledged one other . . . And knowing that had a, an effect on me, like this . . .' In the slowness of her state, she extended a long finger into the flame of my lighter. Even as I watched the flickering light and steady hand, I knew I didn't believe her.

But what could I say, after I'd snatched the bloody lighter back? What could I say when she turned to me and said 'do you not believe me?' It was almost as if she'd said 'did you really not care about me, whether I lived or died?' I must have, I wanted to scream. I want to feel that I did, that's why I need to know why you really wanted to die and why I need to believe there's something more than the life of your vision. Because I don't believe you, Corinne. I think there must be something more. You can't have just been so depressed that the simple fact of not acknowledging someone's presence had that effect on you. I don't want it to be just depression and disillusionment, because then, what'll happen to me? We see things pretty much the same, don't we? So what'll happen if *I* get so depressed that just seeing someone'll freak me out that badly? It couldn't have happened the way she said it.

So I said: 'I'm sorry, Corinne. Jesus Christ, I don't want to be hassling you, but I have to say this. I just don't believe you. There has to be more to it than that.'

'You just never let up, do you?' she said. 'You just keep pushing and pushing.'

'I'm sorry,' I told her again. 'But I need to understand.'

'OK, look, I'll tell you what it was,' she said finally, sounding like it was a huge effort for her to speak. 'He, he wasn't on his own.' Her voice broke down here and then she continued. 'I, I saw him leaving with this middle-aged man, and from the way they looked . . .' she was crying now. 'From the way they looked, I, I reckoned that Shane was on the game.'

'Oh God,' I said, horrified but not particularly surprised. 'Well that's only to be expected, Corinne.'

'But I think it's terrible,' she said, nearly choking. She was in a right state now and her speech was getting incoherent. 'You should have been there . . . I . . . I . . .' She was so hysterical now and crying so much that I was convinced that something else had happened.

'Did you talk to Shane?' I asked her.

Words were coming out of her thick and fast, but I couldn't make them out. I became aware that people were looking at us, so I brought her into the toilets, which were empty, thank God. Eventually, Corinne pulled herself together and we left.

She begged me not to ask her any more questions – it was too upsetting for her. And I felt so bad that of course I left her alone. So we spent her last hours in this city sitting silently in her room, as if we were afraid to break the moment and let events unfold.

But when she was gone, I replayed her words over and over again in my head. Why would Shane's prostitution have made her so upset? If it had been anyone else, I might have understood, but Corinne's hung around with every scumbag in Dublin and she's shagged most of them. It's not as if she's ever been particularly attached to Shane. No, I'd know about something like that. But why else would she be so messed up about it? Because she was so down on herself that seeing Shane confirmed her suspicions that the world was a dodgy place to live in and made her want out? It can't have been that, it can't. That would be too scary. If I only knew what she had been trying to say when she got into that state towards the end. Because there was something in that. In fact, the more I thought about it, the more I became convinced that Corinne must have gone over to talk to Shane and this older man and that something must have happened.

What am I to do, though? I need to know, because then I might be able to understand, and help Corinne. From the state she was in, there's absolutely no way she's over whatever happened. There's no guarantee she won't try to kill herself again. But Corinne certainly isn't going to tell me about it. So that leaves only one alternative.

Four

Hannah wasn't going to be easy. For a start, I hadn't talked to her properly since the night before Corinne . . . And as for what I had in mind . . . Hannah was not going to be easy about it.

'Corinne gone then, is she?' she said, opening the door.

That was another thing: understandably enough, Corinne had been very withdrawn the one time Hannah had called over to see her, and Hannah was obviously still pissed off about that, especially since they used to get on so well.

'Sorry I haven't been over,' I said. 'It's just . . . a lot's been happening, and . . .'

'So you've got loads of scandal for me then? It's well for some, isn't it?'

'Not when it's all bad it isn't,' I answered.

I followed her into the kitchen, and when I saw she had the place to herself, I told her that Corinne tried to kill herself. She was stunned. Couldn't believe it. When she asked why, I started at the surface.

'She broke up with someone,' I said.

'But sure, you never told me she was going out with anyone! Were they going out long?'

I hadn't told her because I hadn't known about it myself. I didn't want to tell her that though, so I pushed on.

'She said that had nothing to do with it. I think she was using it as an example of how she couldn't feel anything emotionally, about him, and about life in general. Only the thing about him was that she tried so hard to make herself care about him that, when she finally gave up on him, she was so confused and hated herself so much that she wanted to kill herself.'

There was silence. And then: 'I don't understand that, Merle. I mean, I can accept what she says and that, but, it doesn't sound like her at all. Corinne always told us she didn't want a proper boyfriend, that she hated all that stuff.'

It was true. I hadn't thought about that in relation to everything Corinne had said, but now that Hannah had pointed it out, it was making me wonder even more about her.

'I didn't believe her either,' I said. 'So I pushed her a bit, and she said . . . Hannah, she said she saw your brother Shane in a pub and that it freaked her out completely.'

The back door had been creaking because it hadn't been closed properly and it was windy. But it wasn't until now that Hannah jumped up and started opening and banging it shut.

'So go on then, tell me what happened,' she said.

'Well, Corinne said she saw him leaving with some middle-aged bloke, and from the way they were acting, she got the impression that Shane was on the game,' I stopped here, wondering how Hannah was taking the news. She was still standing over at the door and didn't speak for a while. Eventually she turned around and said, 'And? What happened next?'

'Well, first Corinne said that she just saw them, but when I asked her if she went over to them, she got so upset that I couldn't make out a word she was saying. But I'm pretty sure she must have, and that something must have happened next, because why else would she have gotten upset enough to kill herself?'

Hannah didn't answer me. The smoky air filled with a heavy

tension, and I got afraid that I wouldn't be able to say what I'd come here for, so eventually I just took a deep breath and said it.

'Hannah, I want to find out where Shane is, so I can go and see him. I want to know exactly what happened that night.'

Hannah slammed the door so hard that she almost shattered the glass.

'Are you off your fucking head or what?' she asked angrily. 'Jesus Christ, if Corinne said nothing happened, then nothing happened! But I'll tell you this much, if you go looking for him, then you could come back here in a nice fucked-up state yourself.'

She twirled and twisted the key in the lock, before turning on the light – it brightened the room, but it showed up the bars on the door and window.

'Why would I come back fucked-up if nothing happened when Corinne saw him? You're not making sense,' I said.

'Well Corinne isn't making any sense, is she? I mean, she had the chance to freak out at the sight of Shane every day of the week when he was living here, but she never did, did she?'

'That's why something must have happened that night, isn't it?'

'No, I mean, if she was depressed about her boyfriend, then that's reason enough to slash her wrists, isn't it?'

'It was actually pills she used,' I said almost silently.

The silence spread over Hannah, making her sit back down on the table.

'Look,' she said next. 'Corinne used to sleep around and stay away from relationships, didn't she? So it's a big deal that she was going out with someone, and I reckon that she did want to die because she couldn't make herself care about him.'

'Yeah. But Hannah, you weren't there when she said it. I was, and there was something so wrong about it that it was just, it was just real weird, Hannah. And you didn't believe this story about the boyfriend until I mentioned Shane.'

'And now you think I'm making excuses because I don't want to know about Shane.'

Yeah, it was so obvious she was that there was no point in saying anything.

'Your timing's pretty bad, you know,' she said after a while.

Yeah. With college coming up, the last thing Hannah wanted was to go dragging up threatening questions about her family when she was trying to cut herself off from them as much as possible.

'Would it help if I told you I was going to college too?' I asked.

'Not anymore it wouldn't,' she said softly, 'seeing as it's because Corinne told you to, isn't it?'

I didn't bother arguing with her.

'So you expect me to go looking for Shane, just because you're going to college, and because you think I owe it to Corinne, seeing as she's your sister, and I like her, and she did something for me way back. Isn't that it?' asked Hannah.

'This wasn't meant to be a fight, you know,' I said, almost regretting that I'd come. A silence fell, and I reckoned it was about time for a subject change. 'Are you still going out with John?'

But that really pissed her off. 'What's that supposed to mean?'

'I'm just asking,' I said, surprised.

'You don't like him, do you?'

'I just don't think you'd be going out with him if he wasn't in college.' I shouldn't have said that, but I did, because I was angry and disappointed.

'Fuck off then,' she said.

I didn't say sorry. For some reason, it didn't seem to fit. I just left.

It was strange she'd say that, about owing Corinne one. She used to say that all the time, but that was years ago, when we were fourteen. What happened was that Hannah got done in by a gang of girls after being with this one's fella. I'd told her he was dodgy, but she thought he was sound, and that he'd broken it off with your one – not that it mattered in the end. We all felt sick when we heard, and Hannah was in a terrible state. But Corinne spent ages with her, talking to her and that, making her feel better. Not only that, but Corinne knew a drummer who was originally from that estate, and she got him to frighten the life out of everyone in that gang, so none of them dared come near us ever again and Hannah wasn't afraid to go out anymore.

I'll never forget how pleased Corinne was when I told her things were working out now, thanks to her. She said that the drummer's band were playing that week, did I want to come with her to see them? Hannah probably wouldn't get in, but I would, especially seeing as I'd be with her, who was now legally eighteen. I'd like them, she said, they were really good, and she'd pay in for me and all.

What could I say? The room was bright from the summer sun, but it wasn't the sun that was responsible for the burning blindness that suddenly hit my eyes. I looked at her, knowing she knew I had good reason to hate her friends, despite what this drummer had done, but all I could see was that she'd be insulted if I didn't go. And I felt I owed it to her to go after what she did for Hannah, so what could I say?

I drank a lot that night before we went into town – I had made Corinne buy me loads, because I needed it, I needed something on me for going in. At that age, me and Hannah hadn't even tried to get into a pub yet, but I wasn't even thinking about being worried about getting in – even if I'd thought about getting out of this gig by being turned away at the door, I'd still have failed Corinne – by being turned away. And when the time came, I just walked in past the bouncer in a daze, as if the thought of my age and getting in past him was not in question.

And then I was finally able to head for the bar to get more drink. I drank a lot, very fast. Corinne didn't seem to notice, she was used to serious drinking, and anyway, she was sitting with a big group of people, talking. I was sitting there beside her, but I wasn't talking – I had such good reasons for hating Corinne's friends that I couldn't bring myself to give this crowd a chance, even though I'd never met them before. Corinne often looked at me and smiled, and I just smiled back. I couldn't talk anyway, talking would have distracted me from proper drinking, and besides, I had an excuse for being quiet when the music started.

There were these fellas sitting beside me. They didn't say much to me, but what they did say was normal enough – of course it was, I had to stop expecting tonight to be a repeat of the last time I was out with Corinne's friends . . . These two fellas were friends of the band on stage, and they were in a band too. I don't remember anything I actually said to them, because I was completely scuttered and didn't register it. And I was trying hard not to make a show of myself – usually, I wouldn't have been hung up on something like that, but I was anxious not to draw attention to myself here with this crowd. Just in case. Because they were friends of Corinne's.

So I slow the drinking right down, look at the band. The singer and drummer are good-looking, the rest are just poseurs, well actually the lot of them are poseurs. Now, now, I told myself, that's not nice. But I can't help it, because I can't see them as anything other than friends of Corinne's. They are bad, though. None of them can play very well, and those macho, violent songs give me the creeps when I hear them coming from the mouth of a friend of Corinne's. So I tell the fella beside me how bad I think the band is when he asks me what I think.

'Ah, you're very critical,' he says, but I can tell he's pleased, even though they're his friends. 'They're not that long together, so you have to make allowances for them.'

'Do you think they're good?' I ask.

'Well now, they're not the best around or anything. But still, they're better than a lot of what's out there.'

And Corinne told me before we came here that you have to be relatively good to be playing places like this, and that I should be taking an interest in these things, I'm the one that plays guitar. There's a good enough crowd here, and they seem enthusiastic enough.

I'm still talking to that fella from time to time. He totally loves himself, but he's harmless enough to talk to. The music is so loud that there's hardly any conversation anyway. And if I'm nice to him, Corinne'll be pleased that I didn't make a show of her by being anti-social. But when I say nothing, I feel totally separate from everything that's happening around me, and that's when I feel most comfortable here.

But because I drank fast earlier, I have a splitting headache from it now – the sort of thump you only get from drink, never from noise, and I feel kind of light-headed all over, like you do when you're dizzy, only I'm not. I smoke and smoke, but not as much as I'd like to – I started out with twenty, but now the packet is nearly empty. Corinne still has some, but it'd be such a hassle getting over to her, seeing as it's so packed in here.

When the band finish up, I think, great, we can go home now. But no, no one seems to be moving. The band wander in and out of the place, packing up their stuff, and then come over to be told how good they were. The lights are all on now, and eventually we all move outside because the place wants to close up. But there's still hanging around talking. And it's dark and cold. I have a headache and I want my bed. I don't want to hassle Corinne though, I'm sure she'll be ready any minute now.

I'm still talking to that fella – though it would be more

accurate to say that he's talking to me. He's not saying much, from what I can remember, but he must be saying something, I know that. Because he's walking a bit away from them, and I have to walk with him because he's talking to me and I don't want to be rude. Eventually, everybody else is a bit of a distance back down the road from us, so I say that I'd better go back, that I have to go home with Corinne. And he says just to go a bit further, and I do, and the next thing I know, I'm in this lane, and he has me up against the wall, snogging the face off me, and I'm thinking, God, how did I get myself into this, but I should have known, what did I expect, him talking to me all night, then being here on my own with him – he is one of Corinne's friends, after all. Don't worry about it, you don't exactly fancy him, but you've snogged worse, it doesn't matter . . . Oh but it did matter though, because he wanted a shag, and I panicked, once it was obvious to me, and tried to get away, but he got rough then, nasty. Said I was a fucking tease, knocked me up against the wall. I hurt my back, worse, my head got a nasty whack, and I was afraid, because it was spinning and hurting me, and I knew that I'd be finished if I lost all control of it, but I managed to get away, I did. And I ran.

I was so relieved when I saw Corinne and them again. I walked up to them, looked at my watch, I'd only been gone ten minutes. Nobody paid any attention to me, and Corinne didn't notice anything being wrong with me. I didn't tell her about it on the late bus home, because what could I say? My heart screamed at her to guess what had happened, but she never copped on.

What could I say? Just because they all went around shagging each other . . . What happened to me was the sort of thing that happened if you went out with Corinne's friends. I spent two nights with them, and two nights was more than enough for me.

That particular night was the first night I sat in my room and cut myself in anger. It was such a relief when the blood came, because it was only then that I allowed myself to cry, which I did with a strange sense of comfort, feeling that I had a right to my pain now. Nobody knew it that night except me, but neither me nor Hannah owed Corinne that particular favour anymore.

And Hannah and Corinne still don't know that, I was thinking, when the doorbell rang. It was Hannah, standing there on the doorstep crying.

'If you're going looking for Shane, then I'm coming too,' she said. 'Whatever happens, I want to be there, I want to see it for myself.'

Silence was the only answer in that tense, heightened peace. From where her eyes fell, somewhere on the ground outside and away from me, her voice fell into the pattern of a prepared speech.

'Obviously I'm not telling anyone at home about this,' she said.

'Neither am I,' I answered.

'In fact,' she said, wiping her eyes, 'I don't want anyone to know – anyone who can't help us, that is. Not telling John won't be a problem because, because I broke it off with him.'

'Oh, Hannah. Why did you do that?'

I did my best to be as sympathetic as possible, though I reckoned it would be a bit two-faced of me to say I was sorry, after what I'd said to her earlier. God, I felt so bad about that now.

'I don't know, because, because I really didn't want to tell him about all this and I thought I should want to tell him. And maybe because I didn't want to believe Corinne about Shane, so I wanted to believe the other stuff instead. I think Corinne's right about relationships when it comes to me and John anyway, because, because it was just so cold, you know, it was just so cold to break it off, just like that. And even while I was actually breaking it off, it felt so cold, only I didn't care!'

'Are you sorry you did it?' I asked, completely stunned by all this.

'No . . . Anyway,' she pushed on, 'that's not what I meant to talk about. I don't know how we're going to find Shane, but I was thinking the best people to talk to would be anyone I can remember being in school with Shane and Corinne. And the only one I can think of, who's probably the best one anyway, is Rob. I know you haven't seen him in ages, but he's the sort of person who might know something, like where to find Shane.'

'I didn't realize that Rob had been in their class,' I said, a bit unnerved and displaced by the fact.

'How come?' asked Hannah, swallowing back. 'Even I know that, and I wasn't as friendly with him as you were.' She stopped for a minute, staring out at the street. 'Anyway,' she said, with business in her voice, 'I'm not working tomorrow, are you?'

'No.'

'So we'll do that, then. Go and see Rob. I'll call over to you. Around twelve.'

And then she was gone, leaving our web of estranged complicity behind her.

Five

It always rains when I come here to Rob's flat. It's strange I remember that, because I haven't been here in two years. And usually, I don't think about the rain.

Rob's in a band and on the dole. He's an absolute ride and I used to fancy him. I'd get on a bus and come up here all the time. I was sixteen then and he was twenty. He was only interested in being friends, but I'd come to his flat anyway. I loved the place, because I'd charged it with the drama of suppressed emotion, and every time I visited, I drew on it, and it stirred me up, so I left on a high.

And today, it was raining in a blue summer sky, so the flat was all lit up with brightness while also being a warm, smoky enclosed shelter. And as soon as I was inside, I felt reassured by the intensity of my memories of the place, memories which I could almost see reflected in the walls and calling out to me.

'I'll wait here,' Hannah had said, standing on the doorstep of the crumbling old house in the pouring rain.

'I thought you wanted to be there when I was talking to him,' I'd said tonelessly, staring at his window three storeys up.

'Well I'm nervous now, and there's no point in that, is there, not when it's only Rob. It's, it's enough for me to have come here, I'd prefer to hear whatever he says from you.'

I didn't push her because she was upset. I left her there on the wet doorstep.

It's weird in here, nothing ever changes. Rob's wearing the same clothes he's always worn, and he doesn't seem surprised to see me, even though it's two years since he's laid eyes on me. I just walk in the door and he says hello, he doesn't even look up from where he's fiddling with his crackling old record-player. This flat's a time warp. The only difference is that he's on his own now. There used to be loads of people here all the time – his flatmate Dermot, the other band members, and all their friends.

'So,' said Rob, sitting on the floor. I noticed that the same old rip was still in the same old place in his jeans. 'You went back to school, didn't you?' he asked.

He was talking about the last time I was here, how I spent the essence of a summer here – more time and emotion on him than I spent on my own boyfriend during those months. And then, when September came, I disappeared. Rob didn't want me to go back to school. He said that school was part of the system, and that all true musicians hated the system, because it tried to crush them, and he didn't want that to happen to me, because I was really good. He'd been saying stuff like that to me since the night we met, at the start of that summer, when he and his friends heard me and my band playing a community centre gig. Rob said not to worry about anything – even if my mam threw me out of the house for leaving school, which I knew she wouldn't, then I could move in with him until I was old enough to get the dole. I'm only sixteen, I told him. 'So?' he answered, 'So was I when I left school.'

The whole idea sat on me like hell, though, because I didn't want to become part of all this. What freaked me out wasn't so much that Rob and them were wasters, it was the fact that they justified their lives on false pretences. They called themselves musicians, and because they believed they were capable of

31

success, it meant that, even if they spent the rest of their lives on the dole, it wasn't their fault that they'd ended up like that – only a few bands made it, and they themselves just weren't the lucky ones. The thing about Rob and his friends was that they never even practised their instruments, and most of them could barely play at all. So no matter how much I liked them as people, I was really uncomfortable with their whole lifestyle – it was like all this music was just an excuse to glamorize their lives. And there was such a strange emptiness in the way Rob talked about and listened to music.

'That was two years ago. I'm not in school anymore,' I emphasized, trying to bring him into the present. Rob must be twenty-two now. The same age as Corinne.

'So what have you been doing with yourself?' he asked.

'Oh, nothing much ... My sister Corinne was home on holiday for a while, do you remember her from school?'

He just looked at me and started tuning his guitar with an electric tuner – his ear was so bad that he could never tell if it was in tune or not.

'Corinn–ah. I do, yeah. We were in the same class in primary school. And she went to college. I remember that.'

'I'm going to go to college too,' I said.

The idea was to use my reasons for going as an introduction to telling him what happened with Corinne, but it was a mistake.

'Why? Did Corinne make you?' he asked.

'Corinne tried to kill herself.'

I walked over to the record-player to turn it up and drown out any vulnerabilities the broken conversation might incite. Standing over the record-player, I couldn't avoid seeing myself in the cracked mirror. They'd knocked it off the wall one night when they were drunk and broken it, and because they were too skint to buy a new one, they stuck it back together again. Then they draped it in silk scarves for effect so that the cracks would look deliberate and sinister, and hung it above the record-player to keep it at a safe distance from them.

I could see Rob in the mirror. He was now sitting on the hideous brown couch which had such big rips the orange foam showed through. It used to be covered in a plaid rug thing that someone's girlfriend gave them, but then she took it back when she found out he'd done the dirt on her. Rob pulled out a pack of tarot cards from under a cushion and started flicking through them. They were dirty and creased. He pulled out the number thirteen skeleton.

'So Corinne chose to play the death card,' he said.

Is this all we're worth? OK, I haven't seen him in two years, but, because we used to be friends, this isn't the reaction I was expecting. No point in getting angry with him, though. Not until I've asked him about Shane.

'That death card doesn't mean death. And anyway, you shouldn't mess with tarot cards, Corinne says they're dangerous,' I told him.

He didn't say anything. I looked around at the decaying walls, wondering why they and Rob were turning against me and pushing me out. The harder the sun shone and the rain fell, the more depressed and displaced I felt.

'Don't you even want to know why she did it?' I asked.

Rob was still sitting there on the couch, flicking through the tarot cards as if I hadn't spoken. 'I suppose,' he said.

'It has something to do with Shane, do you remember him?'

'Oh yeah. What about him?' he asked, deliberately concentrating his attention on the cards.

'Corinne ran into him and this older man in a pub one night.'

Rob dropped the cards on the floor in a violent movement of shock that scattered them all over the place.

'What's wrong?' I asked, stunned by the intensity of his reaction.

'Nothing,' he said scowling. 'I'm just surprised she told you about it, that's all.'

'Why?' I asked, stunned, hoping he'd go on. But Rob didn't answer. I picked up the moon card from the floor beside me. The tension and stress in the room made me lightly scratch the picture with my short, very sharp nails as I examined it. Two dogs wailing in the shadow of a black moon. Rob was there that night. I don't see how else he could know, because I'm pretty sure that Corinne hadn't been talking to anyone I didn't know about in the days after she tried to kill herself.

'So how come you were there?' I asked him.

'How come I was there?' he stared at me. 'Where the hell did you get that idea?'

'I don't know,' I said. 'I just thought, well, that's the impression I got.'

'What exactly did Corinne tell you?' he asked angrily.

'Nothing,' I said, deciding to be straight with him. 'She just said that she saw Shane and your man together and then she was too upset to tell me the rest. But you have to tell me what happened. Please, Rob. Because she's still all messed up about it, and if you tell me, I might be able to help her. Because otherwise, I'm, I'm afraid she'll just kill herself.'

'It's none of your business if she didn't tell you.' Rob said, sullen and closed off.

'Please, Rob.'

'No,' he said.

We sat there in silence for a while, Rob ignoring me, and me trying to figure out what to say. The last match in my box cracked as I was trying to light it. Rob took my cigarette from me. I followed him to the cooker and watched him light it for me in a wave of flame.

'Why won't you tell me?' I asked him quietly.

'Because,' he said tonelessly. I waited for him to continue, but he didn't.

'Well, maybe you could tell me where Shane lives, so I can go and see him,' I suggested.

'I . . . don't know where he is. That wouldn't be a good idea anyway.'

'Why?' I persisted.

'It just wouldn't. Look, it doesn't matter anyway, because I don't have a fucking clue where he lives.'

'Are you sure?' I asked.

'Yes.'

'Well . . . would you know someone who'd know?' I was getting desperate now.

'No, I don't know many people anymore, especially now that I'm not in the band,' he explained quietly.

Not know anybody, not in the band . . . So the Rob I used to know had dissolved into the light and the cracks of the room, leaving only this shadow behind him. I could feel the weight of his isolation and emptiness, and I thought of how he must have spent the last two years drifting aimlessly into a sea of soul-destruction.

'You still play guitar though,' I urged.

'I suppose,' he laid an impersonal hand on it, his lack of expression unnerving me.

'I'm going now,' I said, realizing painfully that there was no point in staying on. 'But Rob, you never hung around with Corinne, did you?'

He had bent over his guitar, so there was no sign of whether he heard me or not. Oh well, I thought, don't worry about it. You'll find Shane some other way, and maybe he'll tell you what happened. I closed his door behind me, and when I walked downstairs, I was pleased to find Hannah in out of the rain. She was sitting on the stairs in the hall, talking to some girl.

'This is Danielle,' said Hannah. 'She's been going out with Rob for six months.'

'Oh, I didn't know he was going out with anyone,' I said, amazed. The Rob I knew two years ago would never have gone out with anyone that long. And he was now a sullen shadow of what he used to be. 'I haven't seen him in ages though,' I added, in case she thought it was bad of Rob not to have told me about her.

'Yeah, Hannah was saying that the two of you came over here to have a look at the college.'

I don't know which struck me first: how near this house was to the college, or the lengths Hannah was going to to avoid talking about Shane.

'Danielle's in her second year there,' said Hannah. 'She's been telling me all about it. Wasn't that great now, running into her while you were giving Rob them tapes back.'

You can tell that Hannah sees sunshine in this girl. I suppose she reckons that if Danielle can be in college and going out with a waster like Rob then maybe she needn't worry so much about having a brother like Shane.

'The only person I knew in that college was John,' said Hannah, getting emotional. 'And I broke it off with him last night.'

Danielle felt sorry for her. Arranged to meet up with us in college next week when we started and show us around.

'Cool,' said Hannah. 'Can I've your number?'

'Where do you live?' I asked.

'Here,' said Danielle, 'myself and another girl are in Flat 3. It's just in there on the right.' She pointed to the top of the first set of stairs.

'It's OK, Hannah I know the number,' I said, staring at the coin box beside us in the hall. I knew it from Rob.

'She's nice, isn't she?' Hannah said when we were outside. 'I

36

couldn't believe it when she said she was going out with Rob. I mean, she's good-looking and all, but he usually just goes for slappers, doesn't he?'

'Why didn't you tell her why we were here? Don't you think Rob will, like, tell her I didn't drop back any tapes?'

But if he wouldn't tell me what I wanted to know, I couldn't see him telling anyone else, even if it was his girlfriend.

'Maybe, maybe not. We'll wait and see, anyway,' she said. A short silence fell. 'So what's the story then?' asked Hannah, nervous again.

'Who knows,' I said. 'You are not going to believe this, but he seems to know everything about Corinne. I mean, you should have seen the way he reacted when I told him that I knew about that night in the pub – he was shocked that I'd know anything about it.'

'No way,' she said. 'So what happened then?'

'Well, I ended up having to admit that I didn't know the details of that night, and as soon as he heard that, he just shut up and said it was none of my business.'

'Oh my God,' said Hannah.

It had stopped raining. But the path was torn up for work on the pipes. Filthy job. If Corinne was here, she'd be in serious pain with all the grit flying into her contact lenses. This was the sort of area that was always getting done up but never actually got there. The sort of place that wasn't very far from town, but too far to walk. Seedy, but without the atmosphere to make it cool. Just grim and old. On our bus route, though. We crossed over to the bus stop.

'So what are you going to do, then?' asked Hannah.

'I don't know,' I said. 'I wish there was some way of making Rob talk, but I don't think there is, though you could ask Danielle if he's ever said anything to her about that night, or even just about Corinne and Shane.'

37

'I'd rather not, if you don't mind. It might embarrass her or something. And she's so nice, she's going to show us around college next week.'

Why would it embarrass her, I wanted to ask. But the bus pulled in then and I lost the moment.

'The only other thing I can think of,' I said when we were sitting down, 'is to look for Shane in that pub Corinne saw him in.'

'I don't like the sound of that. I mean, we can't just sit there like eejits night and day on the off chance he turns up.'

'Why not? Isn't sitting around what pubs are for?'

She didn't answer me.

'Well, can you think of anyone else we could talk to?' I asked her.

'No,' she said, staring out the window where the sky was a calming blue now, so settled. 'Sorry. Like, I want to help you find Shane and that, but I don't want my life any more messed up than it already is.'

'Of course not Hannah, don't worry,' I said, anxious to reassure her. 'All I'm saying is that Corinne saw Shane on a Saturday night, so if we went to that pub on a Saturday night, then it's likely enough he'd show up again, isn't it?'

'Shane? Once or twice in there and he'd have been barred, don't you think?'

'I suppose we could ask the bar staff, they'd remember someone like him,' I said.

'Merle! I'd be mortified.'

'Well, what do you want to do then?'

She didn't know. I didn't know what to say to her, because it was so obvious that she was torn between not wanting to find Shane and wanting to help me out.

'We could just go there for a drink on a few Saturday nights and see what happens,' I said.

She considered this. 'Not this Saturday though. I'm working.'
'Next Saturday, then.'

She sighed. 'That'll be the end of our first week in college. Yeah OK, we'll do that then.'

Six

We started college the following week. Because I was still working, I had barely enough time to catch my breath, and it was all a bit of a blur to me. We saw Danielle every day for lunch, and Hannah smiled each time she saw her. That first day, Danielle was with another two girls who were kind of snotty. They soon disappeared though, and I liked Danielle better when she said that even though they had been the best of friends, they didn't get on with each other as well as they used to. Nowadays, she usually only saw them at work – they all worked part-time in McDonald's.

As the first week went on, Danielle became the focus and symbol of the whole experience for Hannah. So much so that when Danielle mentioned she'd be on her own on Saturday night because Rob had to go somewhere, Hannah couldn't help asking her to come out with us. She told Danielle that we were going for a drink in this pub that was meant to be nice, but she didn't tell her why.

'What did you do that for?' I asked on the way home.

She shrugged. 'I felt sorry for her, sitting at home on her own with Rob gone out. She didn't say anything, but I reckon things must be a bit dodgy between them if he's going off without her.'

True. Especially if he didn't hang around with anyone anymore, like he'd told me. That wasn't the point, though.

'But how are we going to manage it, seeing as you won't even tell her about Shane? What's going to happen if we see him?' I asked.

'It's not going to happen, Merle,' she said softly.

'How do you know?'

'I just do, I have a feeling about it. Anyway, this place is probably jam-packed on a Saturday night, so even if he is there, we mightn't see him, and if we do, then we can just make some excuse to Danielle and go over to him.'

'We wouldn't be just saying hello, you know.'

'So, we'll think of something. If worst comes to worst, you can talk to him on your own, and I'll go back to Danielle.'

It didn't sound very promising. God, I don't know if I'll ever find Shane at this rate, and even if I do, does he have the answers? But something happened that night, why else would Corinne have reacted so badly? Still, maybe my wanting to find Shane has more to do with me than it does with Corinne. I'm so scared by my only reaction to what she did that I need to believe we're different – if there was no serious cause for her wanting to kill herself, then it's likely that I'll drift into an empty suicidal state like hers one day, isn't it?

I got so worked up about the whole thing and so worried about Saturday night, that I made myself play guitar when I got home, even though I didn't want to – I never want to play these days. It brings me to this emotional state where I'm all wound up as if I'm going to cry, only I don't feel like crying, but there's a strange kind of relief in it as well. My room feels reassuring, with its strong, clean colours, its sea-green walls sealing me in – you could call it a cleansing experience after all the dirty concrete outside and the dulled daylight from a skyline darkened by black clouds.

This state doesn't last long, and soon I'm back to thinking about Hannah and how she broke off with John. She still seems to be upset about him, so I feel guilty because I reckon I pushed her to it. This means that, no matter how annoyed I get about her ambivalent attitude to looking for Shane, I won't say a word to her about it. It's so frustrating though, the way she insists on being involved in the whole thing and then reduces the range of options I can use to find him.

I can't sleep tonight, I'm too light-headed. So I'll be up all night with my smokes and the mice that have moved back into the house for the winter. I could sit with the light on, but it would be too claustrophobic. Or I could sit in the dark, watching the curtains blow in the draught and listening to the mice under the floorboards. No, that would be too creepy, even though the sound of a car driving by would make it less sinister. Unfortunately, cars don't come past often enough for that.

But the morning will come, it always does. Even Saturday night comes, with its anxieties and restraints.

Saturday night. We were in that pub at half-six – I insisted on being there that early so we could be sure of a table with a good view. Danielle didn't even comment on how early it was, or how empty the place looked, especially as it was a big, open timbered room, with tables on different levels. I immediately went up to one on a balcony overlooking the door while Hannah went to get the drinks.

'I'd say this place will fill up soon,' I said to Danielle, who was weirdly subdued today. Hannah had been talking non-stop at her all the way down here, so this was the first time I had actually spoken to her.

'I suppose so,' she said, casting an uninterested eye around it.

'How's Rob?' I asked, more to break the silence than because I wanted to know.

'Alright, I suppose. He's gone off somewhere tonight, and I don't know where he is. I can't tell you how glad I was when ye asked me out, because I would have gone mad, just sitting at home wondering what he was up to.'

'We were delighted you could make it,' I said.

'Yeah, well, I could have gone home for the weekend, only that would have given him an excuse for going off without asking me to come with him, and I'm not letting him away with it this time.'

'Does he do this sort of thing a lot?' I asked.

'Oh yeah,' she said, kicking her heels forward and back on the wooden floor. 'Can, can I ask you something?' she said purposefully, pausing for a second before continuing. 'You seem to know Rob quite well, don't you?'

'I used to, but I've only seen him once in the last two years.'

'So would you know if he has another girlfriend?'

I was surprised. 'Well I haven't heard anything about him in a long time, but I doubt it, Danielle. The last time I saw him, he didn't seem to have seen anyone in a while.'

She was pleased with that. 'OK then, I'll tell you everything, and then you can tell me what you think.'

Hannah had come back and couldn't wait to hear it all. I looked uneasily at my watch, thinking how much time this would take. But I could see that Danielle was upset. And besides, it wasn't even seven yet, the place was quiet, and I knew that Corinne wouldn't have been in here this early the night she was here.

'I know he likes me, a lot,' she said.

'Oh yeah?' I said.

'And sometimes things are really cool,' she continued. 'But he gets moody and unpredictable, especially this past month. So there are days when he's a total asshole, and he just sits there scowling, totally out of it. And then, when he does talk to me, he says really mean things like, what kind of an eejit are you, only an eejit would say something like that, even if I was just telling

43

him about a perfectly normal conversation I had with someone, or something that happened at work.'

'How can you take that kind of shit?' Hannah had to say that, true to form. Fortunately, that didn't seem to upset Danielle.

'It's just so weird, the whole thing is weird,' said Danielle. You would have thought she was being defensive were it not for the fact that she didn't seem to have heard or registered Hannah. 'Not only is he so different on his good days, but it's as if he doesn't remember the other days at all. And if I talk about the bad days, then he acts like it's totally natural for him to be like that when he's depressed. He makes me feel that it doesn't really matter what he's like on a bad day, because if I was in tune with him the way I should be, then I'd be depressed too.' She looked at us anxiously.

'He's just selfish, trying to come across as difficult to understand,' said Hannah. 'He's just playing games to make himself feel important.'

'But the whole thing is difficult,' Danielle said warily.

'I'll tell you what it is,' I said. Both of them looked at me. 'I've known Rob a long time, and I reckon he really does like you, Danielle. Because otherwise, he'd have finished with you a long time ago – he enjoys throwing people out of his life, it gives him a sense of power.'

She smiled, both sad and flattered, and looked away in the direction of the bar. Then she took out a cigarette automatically, her head still turned away. Hannah passed over a lighter, touching her sympathetically on the arm to draw her attention to it. She picked it up absent-mindedly and fiddled with it before using it and putting it back down carefully, aligning it with the carelessly slanted cigarette packet. She had an air of glamorous fatality about her, and there was something in this that made me want to reach out and stick a pin in her to show her that she was flesh and blood, make her realize that she shouldn't play up to

Rob, that she should finish with him now before she got badly hurt.

I sat there, scrutinizing everyone that walked in the door in case they were Shane and thinking about Rob and Danielle. Hannah had asked me once or twice during the week if I was jealous of Danielle going out with Rob, seeing as I had never managed to get that far. She should have known better, though. Apart from the fact that I want little enough to do with him after the way he acted the day I went to see him about Corinne and Shane, the summer I spent hanging around with him seems such a long time ago now. I remember it as a time when I was still young and unselfconscious enough to assume that things and people were what they appeared to be and what I thought they must be. It had never occurred to me that Rob had been in school with Corinne – if it had, I probably would have seen him differently; I might have copped on that he was a right prick. But because I was young, and because he was such a fine thing, I saw him as part of a whole backdrop of place and atmosphere, a setting that shone for me with all the colour and promise in the world. Maybe Danielle sees something similar in him. Maybe that's why she wants to stay with him, because it's so much easier to be like that, when there's some kind of excitement to dilute the pain.

The place was filling up, but there were no blond males who looked anything like Shane. Danielle had reached the end of her cigarette. She stubbed it out with a strong, thorough movement, still gentle enough not to upset the fragile balance of my own cigarette, which I'd left resting in the ashtray. It had burnt right down to the end without the ash disintegrating at all – I don't remember ever seeing that before – the long coil of ash usually breaks up at some point, so there's something disturbing about the tense stillness of this one. Hannah looked at me, thinking that someone had better say something, wondering if I was going to finish what I'd started.

'Why is he such a bastard, then, if he likes me?' Danielle asked. 'I tell you, this past month has been really bad. And he keeps going out all the time, he's gone for hours on end, and he never tells me where he's been. That's the main reason why I think he's doing the dirt.'

'It's up to you whether you want to put up with him or not,' I said. 'The way he's acting with you, he wants you around, but you have to be on the same level as him, because otherwise he'll feel insecure and threatened. And the thing about Rob is, I reckon that he thinks he's nothing, so he has to think you're nothing too, which is why he treats you so badly.'

I knew. Even though he used to be so friendly with me, he'd only ever been comfortable with me when he was thinking of all the things we had in common – we were from the same area, both into music . . . But I hadn't left school early, so that had been the end of us being friends.

'It's because you're in college,' Hannah told Danielle. 'It wouldn't bother most people, but I reckon it'd get at Rob.'

Oh Hannah knew what I was talking about alright.

'You make him sound like a total loser,' said Danielle.

'Oh well,' I said. 'Others in the same situation wouldn't come across so bad, because they make the best of what they have and they do things. But he doesn't even talk to people anymore.'

Why is it a huge emotional release for me to say all this?

'There's just something about him,' said Danielle.

It doesn't exactly cancel out all the bad stuff, I wanted to say. But I kept quiet because the pub was quite full now, and I was afraid I'd miss Shane if this conversation didn't finish soon. Fortunately Hannah took over then, talking about her own love-life – emotions ran high, and the two of them got closer and closer.

Soon the place was black with people. I told the other two I'd be back in a minute and squeezed my way to the door to have a look at the queue outside. No sign of anyone remotely like Shane. I was disappointed but unsurprised as I walked back in past the bouncers. This didn't strike me as a druggie pub – its aura was way too bright and shiny, and they seemed to have a tough door policy, turning away anyone loud or likely to make trouble. I could see Shane nicking handbags here alright, but it wasn't exactly the kind of place you'd go touting for business. Unless he'd arranged beforehand to meet that bloke here . . . No, that would be way too organized for Shane. I pushed my way around, keeping an eye out with a keen sense of purpose.

Staring into a cluster of candle-style lights, I could see that this kind of searching was pointless. And Hannah said I wasn't to ask the bar staff about him. How does she expect us to get anywhere if I don't? But Hannah's afraid of getting there, that's the thing. And there's a lounge girl two feet away from me, adding empty pints to a tower of glasses. Let her go, she probably wouldn't know anything anyway, most lounge staff don't stay long in these places. But she had too many glasses, she nearly tripped and fell, and then she paused next to me, waiting for an opening in the crowd.

'Excuse me,' I said. 'I'm looking for someone called Shane. He's a good-looking fella, blond, and about twenty-two. You wouldn't know if, if he's a regular here or anything?'

'You joking me?' she said. 'He could be in here every night of the week and I wouldn't know – it's jammers in here all the time.'

I could see that alright. 'And do you get much trouble in here, then? You know, fighting, pickpocketing and the like.'

She looked at me suspiciously. 'Very little. You get the odd incident – anywhere this busy does. Nothing unusual though.'

Whatever that's supposed to mean. And then she disappeared, with her precarious tower.

I felt kind of low now. I was staring at a picture of exotic turquoise birds on the wall, wondering if birds with clipped wings ever managed to fly, was it to do with instinct and will and all that, when Danielle grabbed me.

'There you are! Oh my God, you are not going to believe what just happened.'

'What?'

'We'd better go back over, quick.'

I rushed over to our table full of expectancy and relief, all of which flowed away when I saw Hannah just sitting there on her own, as if nothing had happened.

'What's wrong?' I asked.

'Hide me quick,' said Danielle, lowering her head and pushing her stool back into the wall. Hannah looked as confused as I was, until Danielle, who'd been scanning the crowds as best she could from her limited vantage point, announced that it was 'OK now, he's gone.'

'Who's gone?' Hannah asked, full of anticipation.

'Oh God,' she said. 'It's a long story.'

Danielle told us how on her way back from the toilets, she saw this alcoholic barman from home who had been chasing her all last summer. It was over a year ago now, but she still nearly died when she saw him in here. I kind of felt sorry for her that she could get worked up so easily, especially in the light of all that Rob stuff she'd told us. But she did know how to milk this barman for drama. She explained excitedly that she'd been able to avoid him tonight because of the crowds, but she hadn't been able to avoid him that summer because he worked in the only half-decent pub where she lived . . . One night, he offered to give her a lift home, and she agreed, because there were three others with her, so she'd be safe enough from him. But then she and her friends got offered a lift by someone else – someone who hadn't been drinking. The barman hadn't been working that night, you see, so he'd been in the pub drinking since the afternoon. And anyway, when he followed Danielle and them outside with his car keys and saw them getting into someone else's car, he lost the head completely and hopped on your man that was going to give them a lift. And then, when the barman copped that in his state he was physically incapable of beating this other fella up, he started screaming and cursing, kicked the car and put his fist through a window.

'What a night, I tell you. If you could have seen what he did to his hand . . .' said Danielle. She and Hannah made faces at each other.

'It must have looked disgusting – pumping blood all over the place,' said Hannah.

'Yeah, apparently it was fucked for ages after that – interfered with his pulling pints, and whatever else he does with his right hand.'

'Danielle!' said Hannah, and we laughed.

'I haven't seen him since that night, that's why I nearly died when I saw him – I'm so glad he didn't see me.'

That's why you put up with Rob then, I thought. He has to be some kind of improvement on that. All the same, Danielle seemed much happier now, and when we said goodbye to her at the end of the night, she told us that she hadn't enjoyed herself so much in a long time.

'No luck then?' asked Hannah as we got off the bus and started walking home.

Her voice had been cheerful, but she sort of looked at me a few times, in the bright of the street lights and the shaded darkness between them, as if she was afraid of what I might have found out, or of what I might want to do now. All I said was 'no luck', but I think something in the way I said it must have made her feel guilty. Not much though, because what she said was 'oh well, we'll go there again next week and see what happens,' even though it must have been obvious to her that it wasn't the sort of place you'd expect to find Shane in. But I was too tired to push her tonight, so all I said was 'Danielle won't go back there after seeing that barman.' But I reckoned I was supposed to be grateful when she said 'the two of us'll go back, anyway'.

Seven

Over the next day or two, I decided that there was one way to find out what to do. You see, the reason I felt free to look for Shane was because Corinne wasn't here. If she had been, I'd have felt guilty about doing it because she had sworn to me that nothing had happened with him. It was the distance between us that enabled me to follow my own instinct. But Hannah had my hands tied so much that I couldn't do anything constructive about Shane without upsetting her, and I didn't know what to do about it. So I thought it might be a good idea to talk to Corinne. I wouldn't tell her what I was up to or anything, I'd just ask her how she was getting on and stuff, and, depending on how she seemed to me, I'd be able to make a decision on whether I should look for Shane on my own terms, leaving Hannah and her conditional involvement aside, or whether I should give up on him altogether.

I couldn't talk to Corinne on the phone at home. Mam was always there, asking her for hours about how she was feeling, was she any better . . . It was so bad that by the time Mam had handed over the phone and closed the door behind her, I felt so oppressed, and Corinne was so drained, that we had nothing left to say to each other.

But there were ways around that. Between the end of my estate and where the shops began, there was a good phone box that didn't get used much, so it was perfect for my purpose. And I wasn't taking any chances on being interrupted, so I decided to wait till around eight on a dark, wet and windy weeknight before ringing Corinne.

'Are you on your own?' she asked, when she picked up the phone.

'Yeah, I'm in the phone box.'

'Can you wait there five minutes? I'll ring you back.'

I held the phone to my ear with the button pressed down, in case anyone else came along and thought I wasn't using it. Held the phone to my ear listening to the rain, and wondering what Corinne was working at now. She always went from one job to another, she liked it that way. She was only about a year and a half out of college, and she was too restless to do anything else, she'd told me. She didn't want to be tied down, not yet, not until she knew what she wanted. Mind you, I had always thought it kind of strange that her restlessness kept her in the same city with the same people. But that was different, she'd told me, a big city was so impersonal that she could still feel as rootless as she liked. And besides, knowing people took pressure off her, so she wasn't obliged to go looking for new people in a fit of loneliness or boredom. I shivered when I thought of her saying that she was always afraid of coming to a bad end. Just then, the phone box shook in the wind and the phone rang.

'You're still alive, anyway,' I said. For a moment, alone in the phone box, I'd gotten the feeling I was calling up the dead.

'Still alive,' she said faintly. 'I'm in a phone box too.' Silence.

'Do you still feel the way you did?' I asked.

'I do. But there's something peaceful about it, as if leaving Dublin has pushed all my anxiety about it far, far away, and not thinking about it makes it stay away. So don't ask me about it. Talk about something else.'

But hearing the distance in her voice seemed to push me away from her. And I needed to break that feeling.

So I asked, 'How do you feel about Shane now?'

'I don't feel anything at all about him. Why?' she answered, calm and emotionless.

'It's just, it's just that . . .' But I couldn't tell her that I didn't believe her, so I said, 'I'm afraid of what'd happen if I ran into him.'

'I wouldn't worry about it. Even you have never been in the kind of state I was in that night, so he'd have no effect on you whatsoever.'

I suppose the need to cut myself and stock up on pain was nothing by her standards. And besides, I don't mean that concentrating on Corinne and looking for Shane had taken my mind off all that, but it had given me a bitter, painful antidote to forcefully apply whenever I felt myself slipping back into that state of mind. I was slipping right now, so I took my key out of my pocket, and scraped it along the phone, feeling cool revulsion at the sound – aversion was the way to react to thoughts like that.

'I'm glad you're feeling better over there, but I wish you were still here,' I said.

'Why, what's wrong?'

'Oh, nothing I suppose.' She's wrong though, she sounds so weird. 'I'm with Hannah in college now,' I said.

'And how's that working out for you? Who else do you see?'

'Rob. Do you remember him? You were in school together.'

I wondered how she was going to react to that. Would she think he'd told me anything? Would she wonder how I'd known to go asking him about it? She didn't know that I used to hang around with him. I regretted that now, because the fact that I'd never told her seemed to intensify the distance between us.

'You're not going out with him, are you? Merle! I know he's

good-looking and that, but I wouldn't touch him with a bargepole.' That expression of horror was the first sound of real life I'd heard from Corinne. I was amazed. Where the hell did this come from?

'Neither would I,' I assured her. 'He has a girlfriend anyway. Her name's Danielle, and they've been going out for six months.'

'He has a girlfriend!' she was really shaken by that. 'No way.'

'Why not? How well did you know him, Corinne?' I asked, intrigued by the extent of her surprise.

'Oh, not well. All I can remember about him from school is that I never liked him. I suppose I just can't believe anyone could put up with him for six months . . . What are you doing with him then, if you don't like him?'

What was the best way of explaining to her without lying too much about what I was up to? It obviously hadn't occurred to her that Rob might have let something slip.

'There's not much I can do about it,' I said. 'You see, Hannah's real friendly with Danielle. I don't like him though, he really freaks me out.'

'Why?'

But I didn't want to go into too much detail about music and the past, about Rob's ghostlike quality and his horrible, skewed ways with Danielle, because that would mean drawing on elements of my life that she had been excluded from.

'He just does. He gives me the creeps,' I said.

'That's exactly how I feel about him. He's twisted, and creepy, and . . . Can you not try and stay away from him then?' She sounded frightened.

It's not that big a deal, I thought, or at least not that intense. Rob's more of a clingy, stale smokiness than a lethal razor edge. I half-wondered if she was going on like this in order to scare me away from him. But there was no way of knowing. I didn't think I'd gotten anywhere further with her. I didn't even know if she was any better or not. I just left the phone box with a feeling that, if I was to get anywhere, I should use my own judgement. And all I could come up with was that, no, Corinne probably wasn't any better, and yes, I should definitely try and find Shane, because if something had happened, then it was important that I find out what it was, to stop my sister becoming a real ghost.

Eight

I waited listlessy for the weekend to come, cocooned by the rain. I couldn't even motivate myself to try and shake off the listlessness, knowing as I did that another Saturday night with Hannah in that pub promised nothing and that I'd want to think up something more constructive to do about Shane.

Hannah came in to Spar on Friday night to see me. I was meant to be working, but I seemed to be spending my time staring at the plate glass doors, which were glistening in the rain, sparkling with light reflections. I projected the shell of my cocoon on to the doors, hoping that when they slid apart in a gust of people and rain and air, my own sleepy, centrally heated cocoon would dissolve too. But it didn't.

'You're going to kill me,' Hannah said.

'Why?' I tried to wake up. 'Don't tell me you're not coming out tomorrow night,' I said, guessing what was up, but unable to make it take effect on my mind.

'I can't. I'm really sorry, but there's nothing I can do about it. My mam's going down the bog to spend the night with her sister, and she's making me come with her because she hates travelling on her own.'

'Can your dad not go?'

'No, why do you think I have to go?' she sighed.

'I'll go out on my own then,' I said, trying to fix on a purpose so that the weekend wouldn't be lost.

'Em, well, there's something else I have to tell you,' she said uncomfortably. 'Danielle rang me a while ago in an awful state – she had a fight with Rob because he wouldn't let her come out with him tomorrow night, and she doesn't know whether to break it off with him or not. Anyway, she was wondering if we'd go over and spend the night with her, because her flatmate's gone home and she doesn't want to be on her own, but she wants to stay in the flat in the hope that he'll feel real scabby for leaving her behind.'

'Hannah, I am not going over there tomorrow night.'

Jesus Christ. I don't want to be mean or anything, but I have to go out looking for Shane. Even if I achieve nothing, I'll feel reassured if I'm doing something concrete about him. And it's not as if Rob's going to be in either – if he was, I wouldn't feel quite so bad about going over there, because, even though I know he wouldn't tell me anything, I could still have asked him stuff about Corinne, which would have made me feel that the night had served some purpose. On second thoughts, no, the night wouldn't have worked like that anyway, because I could hardly have gone asking him this stuff in front of Danielle.

'Please Merle, I'll feel real bad if you don't go. And besides, Danielle's always going on about how nice you were, telling her all that stuff about Rob . . . She says it'd make her feel much better about things if you went over to her.'

'And there's no way I could get her to go back to that pub after seeing your man . . .' No. No chance of a compromise.

'I'm afraid she's not in the humour for going anywhere.' Hannah hesitated. 'Look, I know you're pissed off with me, but you can't go out on your own anyway.'

'Nothing stopping me.'

'Well, I can't guarantee anything,' said Hannah, trying to

make it up to me. 'But we both know we're not going to find Shane in that pub, and . . .'

So she was admitting that now. But I wasn't going to let her get away with it, so I said, 'You don't know that, Hannah. Danielle saw her alco barman there.'

'It's not likely though, is it? Look, I don't have any ideas as such, but, I promise you, if you go over to Danielle, then I'll spend all of tomorrow night thinking about Shane and where he might be. And you never know, my mam and them might let something slip about him when they're talking.'

I don't know what Hannah's expecting to hear – a name maybe, a family secret . . . Probably she's not really expecting to hear anything, but at least she's admitting that we're not going to find him in that pub. And she'll try to think of a better way of looking for him. If I spend the night with Danielle. One night of smoky, clingy conversation about Rob and then . . . Even if Hannah changes her mind and decides to back out, I'll have paid my dues to her and I'll consider myself free to push ahead with Shane. Listlessly, I sensed a breath of fresh air.

Saturday was a dull, stagnant day. With a low grey sky like a heavily crayoned page, and a damp air that promised nothing. The sort of weather you were supposed to be grateful for because there was no rain. Danielle was depressed. She'd gone to the off-licence for both of us, and she'd drunk several cans by the time I got to her place.

'You promised me he wasn't doing the dirt,' she said.

'I said I doubted it. Even so, I can't understand why you're still with him if it's like this all the time.' I started on my first can of Budweiser.

She shrugged morosely, flicking ash into an overflowing ashtray. 'I thought Dublin would be more interesting,' she said. 'We always had great crack at home, it's just that things could get boring, because it was the same people all the time, the same lads, and you could do nothing without the whole world finding out about it.'

'It's the same here, really,' I said.

'It shouldn't be, though. I thought that because it was bigger, there'd be more possibilities, but it doesn't work like that. You have your friends, the people you meet at college and work, and the people you meet through them. And that's it, it's the same set-up all over again.'

'But don't you think it's more open that way, because you get to pick who you hang around with, and things don't have to be about what family you're from, who you hung around with ten years ago, and stupid things you'd rather were forgotten about?' Things don't have to be like that, I thought. It doesn't mean they're not, though.

'It should be different, but it's not,' she said, finishing another can. She opened her bottle of vodka. 'Do you want some of this?' she asked.

'No, I'm grand, thanks. I'll have one of these instead,' I said, taking a second can.

Danielle went to the fridge and got out a bottle of Coke for her vodka. 'Yeah, so as I was saying, you're still tied down to one particular set-up. You mightn't like someone at work, but there's nothing you can do about it if they're on the same night as you. And in some ways I might want to break it off with Rob, but then I think, things would be worse if I did, because what would I do with myself? And I'd have to move out of here then as well, because I'd hate having to see him all the time, so I'd lose a good flat. And not only that, but I'd probably have to get a bedsit on my own.'

I wondered what Danielle would even talk about if she wasn't going out with Rob – still him, probably. And I must say, I don't like this flat. It has a mouldy atmosphere, and I can't figure out why, because it's not a particularly bad flat. It's not great though. There's a brown couch and a good condition tan carpet and fresh enough white walls. Then again, the fridge and gas cooker are old and rusting, and the kitchen sink is yellow and cracked. It's a standard enough mix of reasonable and dodgy. I just hate the place, though. I hate Danielle's and her flatmate's stupid posters of country singers with 'Fine Thing !!' written across the bottom of them in black marker. I have posters myself, but there's something very annoying about theirs.

'It wouldn't be the end of the world if you broke it off with Rob,' I said. 'You'd still have your friends.'

'Yeah,' she scowled, pouring herself another vodka and Coke. 'God, I don't know what to do. Everything's just so boring, and I can't think of a way to make things more interesting.'

It was around eight now. Danielle couldn't find her matches, so I gave her my lighter, and she sat down in front of the television, with the heater on, flicking through the channels, smoking. She was quite drunk by now. We could hear music coming from Rob's flat upstairs. And it was getting louder.

'He knows he's not supposed to play his records that loud,' said Danielle. 'The landlord'll kill him if there's any more complaints about noise in this house.'

'I'd say Rob's gone out by now,' I said. 'That's probably Dermot.' Though I didn't know if Dermot still lived with him.

'Dermot's never here. He just turns up once in a while so that the dole office and the landlord'll think he still lives here, gives Rob a pile of rent money and goes. And I tell you, I wouldn't like to know what he's up to or where that money comes from.' She turned the television off.

So Rob really was as isolated as he seemed. 'What does Rob say about it?' I asked.

'He says he doesn't know anything about it. Who knows, though,' she said. The music got louder again. 'He's not usually that bad. He doesn't want to get kicked out, and anyway, he has earphones, doesn't he?' She went to turn the television back on and then changed her mind. 'I hate this telly, anyway. The reception's shit, and I'm sick of having to hit it every time it acts up.'

So she stayed there, watching me closely instead. Upstairs, the album changed.

'And I wouldn't mind, but that's one of my tapes,' she said. 'And I could be trying to study, or anything. I should be studying, I've done fuck all this week. That is so ignorant of him. Do you not think he's ignorant?'

I didn't answer her. I was too busy reminding myself of all the reasons I was here.

'I tell you, I've a good mind to go up there and ask him when he's going off to his other girlfriend so that the rest of us can have some peace and quiet,' she said.

'Don't,' I said.

Downstairs, the phone started ringing. I looked at her. She ignored it. It went on. 'I'll get it,' I said, wanting to get out of that room. I opened the door. The darkness streamed into the room, and I stood a minute, trying to orient myself to facing the unlit stairs. She followed me to the door, looking down and up. I went downstairs, turned on the light and picked up the phone. But it went dead as soon as I held it up to my ear.

Upstairs, I heard a door open, the music getting louder. Rob's door was unlocked and now Danielle's gone in to him, I thought. I sat on a step and waited. There was a heavy silence – she must have taken her tape back, at least. Smashed the speakers? No, no crashes. Nothing. I stood up and heard the steps creaking beneath me. I flinched at the sound and then leaned against the wall, waiting. But I heard nothing more. So I got impatient, headed up the stairs and went in to them.

It looked as if they hadn't heard me coming – I thought they'd have heard me, what with all the creaking stairs, but no. Rob was lying on the couch, arms crossed, legs crossed, staring up at the ceiling. Danielle was standing at that bloody stereo, holding the tape in one hand and clenching her other fist. Neither of them had done anything yet – each seemed to be waiting for the other to start the confrontation. As time dragged on, they had probably begun to feel a bit stupid, angrier for feeling stupid, and more determined not to be the first.

Maybe they had heard me coming up the stairs and waited for me. Or else my presence made it necessary for them to act. They couldn't hold it off any longer. Either way, that was when the fight started.

She called him a fucking ignorant bastard. 'And I know you have another girlfriend, so you can just fuck off, alright?'

He didn't even look over. He just stretched out, picked up the chair beside him, banged it on the floor twice, and then held it up, pointing it at her. She stared at it, broke off what she was saying and moved towards me. I didn't flinch.

'Shut the fuck up and get out,' he told her quietly and evenly, putting the chair back down softly.

Danielle looked at me, wondering what to do. I looked away. She could do what she wanted, I wasn't getting involved.

I don't think she knew what to do. But she was afraid to move without having made some kind of a decision, so she kept looking around the room for a focus. Looking anywhere except at him. She went over to the mantelpiece, picked up some coins, his keys and a bus ticket. She read out the ticket: 80p, adult, to go to some stop I didn't recognize. It was dated a month ago, but that didn't seem to register with her. This was all she could think of. 'Is this where she lives? So you get the bus out to her house, then, do you?'

'I never get the bus anywhere. I walk and walk everywhere,' he said tonelessly.

'Well whose bus ticket is it then?' she asked, kicking the poster that was stuck over the grate. It ripped and she hurt her foot. Cursing, she tore the poster off, revealing a grate full of maps and bus timetables that had been torn out of the Independent Directory. 'So where does she live?' screamed Danielle. 'You've got the whole fucking city here, you sad bastard.'

'I have to burn something when it gets cold,' he said.

Then he picked up the chair again and this time, he threw it at her. It missed her, but only just. She grabbed the dusty acoustic guitar beside her.

'Don't throw that,' I shouted.

Rob didn't move. She threw it and I went to catch it. Too late. I picked it up from the floor, and as I did, a small piece of paper fell out of it. I unfolded the page: it was a map from the Independent Directory, folded into oblivion. But all its streets had been obliterated with a heavy black marker which had seeped through the back of the page, obscuring the streets of the map on that side too, as if in an attempt to wipe every one of them from the face of the earth. All except one street that had been left clear. 'No. 6' was written at the top of the page.

Danielle grabbed it. 'But you're not burning this map, are you? Just in case you might forget your girlfriend lives at No. 6!'

'It's not a fucking girlfriend, I'm telling you!' he screamed. 'It's a fella from school. Merle knows him too. His name is Shane. Shane! It's not a fucking girlfriend! It's Shane!'

My hands were shaking, but I managed to prise the map away from Danielle. 'Listen to me, you fucking gobshite,' I said to him. 'Are you telling me that this is Shane's address? Even though you told me last time I was here that you didn't know where he lived?'

He shook his head from side to side as if bewildered. 'I didn't know anything about him. I don't know anything about him,' he said.

'But you know where he fucking lives!' I screamed.

'I do, yeah, I do,' he sounded dazed.

'And you know what happened to Corinne that night in the pub, so why the fuck won't you tell me about it, Rob?'

He tried to stand up, but he couldn't, he swayed and fell back on to the couch. He was probably out of his fucking mind on something. Danielle started crying. I looked at Rob and saw that he saw her. He was upset, out of his depth, didn't know what to do. Caught my eye and looked steadily down at the floor for a few seconds before going over to her.

'Are you telling me that's a fella's address?' she sobbed.

He was silent for a moment. Then he said, 'Yes,' very softly.

'And do you promise me that you've never done the dirt, that you've never been with any other girl all the times you were out?' she asked.

I watched, silenced by what I was seeing. Nothing would change, they'd just fuck each other up more. I clung to the rawness of the piece of paper – she doesn't care that he lied to me about Shane, she doesn't even want to know who he is. All she cares about is being his girlfriend. And fuck him too, why does he have to be such a bastard? What does this map mean? I won't find out tonight, anyway, not with Danielle. How much do they really care about each other, I wondered. I don't know, and I don't want to care anymore. There's a terrible darkness in the whole thing, in this room, and I don't want to feel it anymore, don't want to see it.

This is the end of the line for me. I can't stay here, no matter what answers I need. I can't stay here, the darkness will numb me, chill me right through.

It was cold outside. A bitter hard night cold. Freezing, but soothing, because it was so alive, vital, not like in there.

But what do I do? The map was burning a hole in my hand. Visit Shane? I shivered. Do you visit vampires at night? I looked at the sky, wanting to smother the moon, but I couldn't find it through the smoky clouds. I clenched my fists, trying to clear myself of the stupor that even infected the area surrounding Rob's flat. Things never change around here: there's a car with a broken car alarm that's always parked in the same place on that road, and the alarm is always going off. So I stand on the path outside that house, and I can hear the alarm coming from the same place it always is. And now I focus on that sound, follow it up to the car and listen to it fade behind me. I relax only when it's gone. I get to the bus stop, but there's no way of knowing when a bus is going to come. At least they're unpredictable. I'm relieved, because otherwise things would be a bit too freaky.

Bus. I can't go anywhere yet! I don't know what to do about Shane. I'm not going near that place he lives in tonight – I'm not ready. And I can't go without Hannah, I promised her. Does that matter? Yes, it does. Ironically enough, it was her lukewarm approach and her friendship with Danielle that landed me the address. And what do we say to Shane, anyway? My shaking hand held the map up to a street light. Sure what am I talking about? I can't even tell where that road is, so I'm going to have to match it up with a map at home. That'll be easy though, we should be able to go and see him tomorrow. If Hannah's back before dark.

But I don't want to go home yet, I can't. And it's not late, there's loads of people around. I'll stay here, I'll walk and walk, and let the cold wipe me out. I'd rather it was the cold that did that. I like it, I understand it.

Nine

Later that night I got home, numbed to the core. I was blinded by the light in the kitchen and I tingled from the warmth.

'I thought you weren't coming back tonight,' said Mam. Her voice was careless and happy. I blinked, having expected the claustrophobic anxiety that had followed my every movement, ever since Corinne.

'No, well, Danielle has a bad cold so we decided to call it a night. So what's the story?'

'Your sister's here, upstairs asleep in bed.'

'Corinne's back?' I was shocked. 'What happened?'

'Nothing really. She said she was tired and a bit depressed, and that something you said to her on the phone during the week made her want to give up work for a while and come home for a rest.'

What could I have said to her on the phone that night in the phone box to make her come back? Nothing, really. She said she didn't want to talk, because talking to me about what had happened was like being here: it made all the confusion and turmoil crawl back into her and pull her down into some cold dark whirlpool.

'You're very quiet,' said Mam. 'Why didn't you tell me you rang her? I don't mind, you know, if you want to talk to her on your own.'

'Oh, well, she didn't have any news, really. We just had a bit of a chat, and I told her we missed her and that.'

'Well, I'm glad you did,' said Mam. 'And it's good to know that it's us she came to see when she needed to get away.'

Mam would say that, because it meant that we had nothing to do with any of Corinne's unhappinesses, so Mam didn't have to feel guilty anymore. And of course, it would seem totally natural to her that Corinne would come back. But then, anything Corinne did always seemed totally natural to her, even though Corinne never made any sense to me. She only ever made sense in pieces, and even though the few pieces of her that she did reveal to me fitted her – like those melancholic conversations and attitudes – they were only pieces, always part of something else that she kept hidden from me, so much so that I never quite believed her and never quite understood her. I wondered if she would make more sense to me after I met Shane.

'Mam, do we have the Independent Directory?'

'Yeah, it's around somewhere. Why?'

'I just want to check the buses.'

I found it, took it upstairs, and easily matched Rob's map up with the map in our Directory. Shane lived in an area full of big old houses – he must be in a flat then, or else squatting somewhere. What am I going to do about Corinne, though? Obviously I can't tell her about any of this, but I can't very well just go off with Hannah to see Shane tomorrow afternoon, either. And I'm not capable of lying to her about where I'm going. What's she doing here, anyway? The tension and anxiety built up throughout the night.

It was raining the next day. I was sitting in the kitchen, smoking and drinking tea and waiting for Corinne to wake up. It was one in the afternoon. Leave her, Mam had said, she had a long day yesterday, what with all that travelling and everything. But I was beginning to be afraid that Corinne would be too late getting up and I wouldn't get to talk to her while the house was empty.

Eventually, I heard her moving around upstairs. Then I heard the shower going on.

Her hair was still wet when she came in. She filled up the kettle at the sink and stood there for a while, staring out at the rain, the patio, the empty clothes line blowing in the wind. She looked kind of separate to all this, as if she wasn't really here. Disconnected, worn out, but alive. Corinne was still there, all of her, but she was more sculpted than ever, as if her flesh was being chiselled away into edge and shadow. I pinched my arm – I had never gone that thin.

'We'd better bring in them clothes pegs, they'll be ruined in the rain,' she said.

'They're only fucking clothes pegs.' I answered.

What does she care about clothes pegs? She shrugged, put the kettle on, and sat down.

'That's a nice tea towel,' she said, looking at a yellow and green one on the back of a chair. 'Is it a new one?' I nodded. She looked around her: 'Yeah, it's nice. It matches the kitchen and all.'

Next she'll say it's a nice kitchen. I'll strangle her if she does. Nothing against the kitchen, I like the kitchen. But I want to talk to her properly, I want her to tell me what she's doing here.

'Where's Mam?' she asked.

'She said she was going to Dunnes after Mass.'

'Oh. Is she doing the shopping? Did she not need a hand? I'd have gone with her.'

'No, she did it the day before yesterday. But when she was there, she saw a dress she liked in Dunnes and she's gone back to get it.'

'Oh, right. Is it a nice dress?'

I sighed. 'Yeah, it's alright, I suppose.' And before she could ask, I told her, 'It's red, and down to her knees, with big gold buttons going right up it. And it's loose, with a high neck, and it's a sort of woolly material.'

'Sounds lovely, is it expensive?'

'It is for Dunnes, but she says it's worth it, it's good quality, and she'll keep it for real good. And it'll be Christmas in a few months anyway, so . . .' I looked at her. 'Are you staying till Christmas, or are you going to go away and come back again?'

She wasn't looking at me, she was staring at the table and messing with the sugar bowl.

'I don't know. I might well stay here, I'll have to see, fix up about money and all that kind of stuff. There's another girl staying in the flat until Christmas – Maeve's cousin – and I said she could have my room until then, so . . .'

'You mean you'd really stay here that long?' I couldn't believe it. Corinne got up quickly to make a cup of tea.

'Yeah, why not? So how've you been since I was here last?'

At that point, my cup slipped from my hand and dropped on the floor, smashing to pieces.

'That's how I've been,' I said, pointing at the cup.

I could see that she was shaken up, deep down, but she wasn't going to show it – showing nothing meant she had control over what she wanted to keep hidden.

'For fuck sake, Merle, that was a good cup,' she said.

'No, it wasn't. And anyway, it doesn't matter whether it was or not: them cups are a pound in Dunnes and fifty pence in the Pound Shop. Everybody has them. We have them. It's no big deal.'

On the one hand, I was being defensive because I felt I had to justify myself, and on the other hand, I didn't really care about the cup. I hadn't meant to break it, but now that I thought of it, it was a very appropriate thing to do, because it summed every-thing up.

'You asked me how I was, and I told you,' I said. 'I kind of feel like everything around me is smashing to pieces.'

Corinne shook her head and went about cleaning the mess up, as if wondering when I was going to stop acting like a kid. She might have a point there.

'Sorry,' I said. 'I didn't really mean that. I'm just tired, what with work and college and everything.'

Corinne was clenching a big piece of the cup in her hand. She let it go and picked up a few of the smaller ones. One of them cut her. She cursed, said she should have swept them up instead. She should have, come to think of it. She obviously wasn't thinking straight. She sucked her finger, and then came over to me, pulled at my sleeve.

'When you used to cut yourself, did you go far enough to scar?' She ran a finger up my left arm. 'I've often wondered about that.'

The whole room was on edge. I stared back at her.

'No. I suppose I hoped that maybe, one day, I'd get over all that, and I didn't think I'd be able to forget so easily if there were scars there.'

'Oh,' she said, wrapping her finger up tightly with tissue. The blood kept coming through it. 'I was wondering about that. Because that night, the night I tried to kill myself, I resented you, because you seemed to be able to deal with things easier than I could. In fact, I couldn't even decide what way to die, but in the end I decided that pills were a cleaner option. Apart from anything else, I didn't want to mess up the outside of my body, I just didn't. I wanted to keep it as intact as possible. So I thought of you again, and I wondered how much we had in common and if you felt the same about scarring. I was sorry I hadn't asked you.'

She went to the sink, held her finger under the running water. She turned the tap on full, so it came pouring down in a rush, like a small spring in the rain. It made me remember how, when we were kids – when I was four or five and she was eight or nine – we always wanted to know why witches weren't allowed to cross running water. At the time, all we were interested in were witches and vampires, even though we were too young to be allowed to watch the good horror films. Oh God. Look what we've come to now. The state Corinne's in is a lot more frightening than any of that.

'Corinne, did you ever find out why witches couldn't cross running water?'

'Someone told me it was to do with water being God's gift of life, but I don't know if that's true. I meant to tell you that, did I never tell you?' she asked.

Corinne looked tired. I'd noticed that before, but I hadn't realized just how tired she was until now. It was as if she could fall to pieces at any minute, as if she was only being held together by her clothes. She sat down and laid her head on the table. I was surprised to find myself acknowledging the fact that she never cried. I don't think I've seen her cry in years.

'I'm sorry about the cup and you cutting your finger on it,' I said.

'Don't worry about it,' she said, grasping her finger. 'I shouldn't have picked up the pieces, anyway. I wasn't thinking straight.'

The rain was lashing heavier, banging the window, and the sky was even darker than before. But I didn't want to turn the light on because I felt as if I couldn't move from my chair and because I thought the light bulb would make the day look worse, not better. Corinne listlessly poked the pile of ashes and butts in the ashtray with my lighter, cutting and crosscutting them into little sections. I took out another smoke. Corinne lit it for me before going back to what she'd been doing.

'Why did you come back, Corinne?' I said, asking the question I'd been wanting to ask all day.

She didn't look up from the ashtray, but she did speak: 'After talking to you on the phone the other day, a number of things hit me. And I realized that, even though I thought I'd pushed away all the confusion and despair, I was actually just ignoring it and it was still there as much as ever. And I still wasn't connecting with things emotionally, I was just going from day to day, totally spaced out and doing things automatically.'

She pushed the ashtray away sharply, pushed her chair back from the table and crossed her legs viciously.

'It was all so fucking stupid, you know,' she said. 'I even went to a counsellor, and all. And I was sitting there, thinking, well this is a fucking cliché of a scenario if ever there was one, and how the fuck did I ever manage to get myself reduced to this. It's a bloody waste of money, because I'd rather be talking to the wall, the wall can respond any way I want it to, not like this woman with the horrible, heavy perfume that reminds me of sitting next to an oul wan at a funeral.'

Corinne was almost laughing to herself. Almost, it had too hard a quality.

'And this one was sitting there in front of me, trying to relax me,' she continued. '"I'm sorry, I can't do this," I said. "I can't talk through this stuff, it's all I've got to myself." Of course she pounced on that, saying calmly: "Oh. What stuff is it you can't talk through?" "Sorry," I said, standing up. I wasn't sorry, I just wanted to get out of there politely. "That's alright," she said, nodding the head and smiling, trying to disguise the fact that she was more than likely glad to be rid of me, "you come back when you feel you're ready to talk about this stuff."'

Corinne went to the window again. 'Can we go out for a walk? We'd be on our own. It's pissing rain so much we wouldn't run into anyone, and even if we did, they wouldn't stop to talk.'

'We're on our own here,' I answered.

'But I want to walk in the rain. I'll be able to talk to you better.'

Yeah. In the rain, it was as if nothing mattered, so it was easier to say things. And I think it was easier for Corinne that I couldn't see into her face while she was talking. She looked ahead of her as she walked, with the wind blowing wet hair everywhere.

'I was worried about you, you know,' said Corinne. 'I was afraid you didn't like college and stuff.'

It looked like Corinne wasn't ready to talk properly yet, and I didn't want to hassle her, so I answered: 'College is like school. You don't think about it, you just do it.'

'Do you like it though, because you don't sound like you do.'

'Oh, I don't really think about it much.'

'You have to think about something though,' she said, anxious and brittle. 'What do you think about? Music?'

Yes. Sometimes. Most of the time not properly. It's just something that's always there in my head. Sometimes it's the only thing there, and that's the best, because that's the closest I've got to peace during the last week – all of that waiting to go looking for Shane in the pub was very tense, unnerving. And it's almost worse, now that I've the address and don't know what to do about it. I stood still. Just thinking about that map had stirred my blood up, and I felt hot and shaken all over, even though standing still in that wind and rain was actually freezing.

'Are you OK?' Corinne asked, turning back to look at me.

'Yeah, of course I am,' I said.

She didn't look convinced though, and said with horror and unsurprised fatalism: 'Jesus Christ, Merle, I knew I was right to be worried about you when you told me you were hanging around with Rob and that you were completely freaked out by him. That's the real reason I came back, you know.'

'What, to protect me from Rob?' I asked, completely surprised.

73

He needs protecting from me, more like. Though she's probably only saying this so that I won't go over there asking him questions about her. What's she trying to hide?

'To protect you from yourself, of course,' she whispered calmly, giving me the creeps.

What's she talking about? It really is as if there's something about Rob that she doesn't want me to know. There's some connection between the three of them that they don't want anyone else to know about. Why not? A bus had just pulled off ahead of us, leaving an empty bus shelter. Corinne rushed into it and leant against the glass, staring out at the road and the estate.

'Poor Mam,' said Corinne. 'Does she ever say anything about Bernard?'

'No.'

'Because she must be thinking about him a lot.'

'Yeah,' I said, wondering why she had brought him up all of a sudden.

Bernard was Mam's sister's only kid, and she used to be really strict with him and not let him out of the house. Mam used to tell her to go easier on him whenever she saw them, which wasn't very often – her and her sister didn't get on with each other. Mam said that, when he was little, he was a nice, outgoing, lively kid. But as he grew older, he seemed to turn in on himself.

The only time he got away from his mother was the summer when he was thirteen – she let him go to the Gaeltacht to learn Irish. He got sent home a week into the course for sneaking out in the middle of the night to go drinking with two girls. The rest of that year, she said he wasn't allowed out of the house at all except for school, so they had terrible, terrible fights, even in front of Mam. And then he used to do things like rob money from his mam's purse and go out anyway. And things went from bad to worse until he ended up dead from heroin.

Mam took it very hard. She blamed her sister with a vengeance for having given him a miserable life. She destroyed him, Mam said, because if you're too hard on your kids, then they end up running wild once they get away from you.

He died in July. I was six and Corinne was ten at the time. Eventually, I couldn't even remember him properly, but every year, on the anniversary of his death, the three of us would go and put flowers on his grave, and I remember those days very clearly. There was always some blue sky, those days in July. I remember the year I was eleven and Corinne fifteen: some white clouds, strong wind, sun coming in and out... It was my favourite kind of day, but only if you were running around, playing chasing or something, and the three of us had been standing still for twenty minutes at the grave. Me and Corinne were cold, but we felt compelled by the occasion not to move. Mam had on a new white dress she was very fond of, and the night before, she'd asked us to wear our white jeans. Corinne's were cool and tight, but mine were baggy, and they annoyed me because they looked like kids' jeans. At least I was big for my age. Soon I could dress like Corinne – all my friends were jealous because I had a proper bra. She was wearing a tight white top, which was very low at the front – it didn't fit me yet, but I was wearing an old white shirt of hers, and I was happy enough with that.

We put a big bouquet of white lilies on the grave. We always did. Because lilies look so strong, Mam said, like they're going to last.

White clothes, white lilies, and the white lemonade Mam used as a mixer all that afternoon out on the white plastic patio chairs. Call it white lemonade, but you can see through it like you can see through Mam's tears – she cried as she rambled on and on for hours about Bernard and his mother. That was the day Corinne asked her to bring her to the doctor to get the pill. I heard her from behind the back door, and I pressed myself into the curtain on the back of the door to listen in. I inhaled the curtain, it tasted of dust and dry throats. Corinne said she was fifteen and she'd held out long enough. She said she'd been with a very nice boyfriend, her own age, for three months. Mam didn't say anything. The sun went in for a minute, I closed my eyes and when I felt the sun coming out again, I decided it was time to go back into the garden.

I sat down and stared at the ground. It was exciting knowing something I wasn't supposed to. Mam was talking. She'd drunk a lot by this stage, and Corinne had got her timing perfect, as usual – she got her at the stage when she was drunk enough to agree to anything you asked her, but sober enough to remember afterwards what she'd agreed to.

'My sister was always very stupid,' Mam said. 'She never knew how to cope with anything, and she was always getting stupid ideas into her head.'

I was watching Corinne, because she always knew how to get Mam to tell us things she didn't mean to. But Corinne didn't seem to be interested in what Mam was saying.

'Because kids'll find a way of doing what they want anyway, no matter what you do,' said Mam. 'And things are very different, these days. You never know what you should be doing with your kids.'

Confused and emotional, she looked over at Corinne, who just sat there looking back at her. I was delighted to know something about Corinne that she didn't want me to know, because even though I looked up to her a lot, the fifteen-year-old Corinne didn't exactly want her little sister hanging out of her all the time, knowing all her business. So that meant that we'd fight and stuff. And then Corinne would bribe me to leave her alone and to keep my mouth shut. Because there was an awful lot of damage I could do: I could give certain information, such as who fancied who, to the wrong people, and as well as that, certain mams of certain friends would kill them if they knew what they were up to. So this meant that I could make Corinne give me the things I couldn't get off Mam – us two were spoiled rotten, Mam always gave us what we asked for. And so, the big sister who didn't have any time for me would get rid of me by leaving me with the bittersweet consolations of smokes, almost-used-up foundations and lipsticks, and blunt stubs of smudgy eyeliner. And me and Hannah would take those cigarettes, mind them carefully so they didn't break, and practise smoking whenever we got a chance.

Mam was making smiles of resignation into her glass: 'Yis can do whatever yis want, girls. I don't mind, as long as it's not drugs. And if yis ever need anything, or if yis ever need to tell me stuff, I won't mind, whatever it is.'

She looked hard at Corinne, appealing to her. I've always wondered if she ever even tried to understand Corinne, because Mam just accepted everything we did without ever questioning it. Bernard had left too deep a mark.

Mam laughed drunkenly: 'I worry about you, you know, when you're out getting drunk on the side of the road. The thought of anything happening to you, of you being knocked down by a car or something. And it must get cold, being outside in the middle of winter. If it was up to me, I'd invite yis all into my sitting room. I'd be a lot happier then. Only it wouldn't be cool for you anymore, would it?'

Corinne said nothing, just waited for all this to pass. And we sat out there a long, long time.

The sun always set through Mam's bedroom window. It was always very bright and warm in there on a summer's evening. The following day, Corinne was lying on Mam's bed, talking to someone on the phone. I could hear every word.

'Yeah,' said Corinne. 'It was all straightforward enough, we were only in there a little while ... there wasn't much the doctor could say, was there, my mam was with me ...'

I walked into the room, picked the magazines up off the floor and sat down to read them – I wanted to annoy my sister because I knew she didn't want me there. These were all Corinne's magazines, and they were full of articles like 'Ten Ways to Improve Your Sex Life' and 'Keeping Your Man Where You Want Him.' I could smell that she'd been spraying a lot of Mam's good perfume around the room. Corinne told me to get out, but I just smirked at her.

'Do you mind, I'm trying to have a private conversation here,' she said.

'Mam's going to kill you for wasting all that perfume,' I said. Corinne just looked at me. 'Anyway,' I said. 'I know you're only talking about the pill.'

'Oh fuck,' she said, laughing, and got off the phone. 'You're a mad little thing, aren't you?' She kept on laughing for a while, with a laugh that I didn't understand. 'There's no flies on you, is there?' she said. 'Oh well, as long as you know when to keep things to yourself.'

'Do you?' I answered back.

She eyed herself in the mirror. 'Oh you'd be surprised,' she said. 'In fact, I can beat you any day for knowing things I shouldn't. You know, I'm going to tell you something, just to prove it. Something I heard exactly this day, four years ago, when I was the same age as you. We'll see if you can keep a secret.'

I remember now that Corinne got kind of superior and detached. But she seemed a bit frightened as well, as if she didn't understand what was going on inside of her.

'Do you remember Mam talking about how stupid Doreen, Bernard's Mam, was?' she asked, blowing smoke rings at her image in the mirror. 'Well, what Mam meant was that, when

78

Doreen was young, some fella got her pregnant and then ran off to England or somewhere. So she had to get someone else to marry her and she pretended that the baby was his. And that baby was Bernard.'

I didn't know whether to believe her or not. You never knew where you were with Corinne. I just listened, not understanding why she was telling me all this.

'And nobody ever knew about this, except Mam. Doreen told her, soon after Mam got married. She was probably feeling sorry for herself when she saw that Mam's life was working out after she'd ended up being stuck with the wrong man.'

'Who told you that?' I asked, stunned. I don't know if I was surprised – I could believe anything, especially anything to do with Bernard. Corinne turned around on the bed so that she was looking at the ceiling and away from me.

'Doreen came to see Mam, the day after the first anniversary of Bernard's death. We were sent out of the room, and you went to watch kids' programmes on the telly, but I sneaked back, to listen at the door. You see, I was nosey, just like you. Anyway, I heard her telling Mam all this stuff about when she was young and how she really needed to talk about it, and so on. Then she started saying how Bernard had ended up as bad as his real father, and that lately, she'd been considering telling her husband the truth, so that he'd at least know it wasn't his blood that brought shame on them.'

'That's a bit much, isn't it?' I said, trying to sound experienced, like I knew what I was talking about.

'Why? Anyway, I came away at that stage, so I don't know what happened next.'

I remembered that day. I was happy because there were two episodes of my favourite programme on and Corinne didn't fight with me about changing the channel. Not only that, but she even watched it with me, which I thought was kind of unusual because she hated it, but I said nothing.

'Well,' I said, 'why didn't she just have the baby by herself? She was old enough, wasn't she?'

'I thought about that,' she said. 'So one night, I asked Mam what would have happened when she was young if a girl got pregnant. And she said that if that happened to a girl, then that was the end of her. Her own family wouldn't want to know about her. But Mam said not to worry about it, that nobody need get pregnant these days.'

Corinne got up and started brushing her hair, catching it in the sunlight to see how it looked. I didn't say anything, I didn't even move.

'Poor Mam,' she said. 'She doesn't have a clue about anything, really. Still, it means we can do whatever the fuck we want.'

She said that cold and hard, and I was frightened. But now, when I thought about the things she'd said that day, what struck me about them was her preoccupation with pain. And how she had brought all this up at this moment in time to distract me from the present.

The rain was so bleak – all my senses could register was the sound of it on the bus shelter above us. Even when the odd car went past, I didn't hear it because I was watching the drops falling off the corner of the roof instead of the road. I lit up. Even the flame of the lighter looked cold, as if it wasn't going to light.

'Would ya ever give us one, love, go on, will ya?' There was a towering old drunk with a big, shaggy beard standing over me, trying to scrounge a smoke. He was filthy and smelt disgusting, and I was about to get rid of him when Corinne screamed. He smirked, 'Did I give ya a fright, love?'

Corinne ran. I followed her, faster and faster, until she turned up into the dangerous short cut. The one you weren't supposed to use on your own at night. My nails almost tore into my palms, I was clenching them so hard. I looked anxiously up and down, taking in the discarded beer cans, condoms and syringes, but thankfully, there was nobody there apart from us.

Corinne started to laugh and turn round and round in circles. My head swirled trying to follow her movements. Rain exploded all around her.

'I have to sort all the shit out, once and for all,' she said. 'And I know it's all rooted in everything that ever happened to me in this city. And you have to do the same – otherwise neither of us'll ever be able to do anything real. That's why I'm going to go to places like this, places I used to be afraid of, just to show myself that I can see them differently now. Because it's no good just thinking you can see something differently, you have to actually go there in person: only being there can change the images in your head – images of being smothered and burnt and poisoned by men in grey jumpers wanting cigarettes off you.'

'He wasn't wearing a grey jumper, Corinne,' I said. And he didn't touch you, either, I thought. 'Corinne, what's wrong with you, what are we doing here?'

But she didn't answer, she just pointed to everything around her in a wide sweeping gesture and dizzily leaned against the wall.

I hadn't meant to just come out with it, but I was so worried about her, I couldn't help myself: 'Corinne, are you sure nothing happened when you saw Shane that night?'

'Why do you keep asking me that?'

'Because I . . . I managed to get hold of his address in a very weird way, and me and Hannah were thinking of going to see him.'

Corinne said nothing. She didn't even ask why we wanted to make contact with him after all these years.

'Do you know if him and Rob knew each other well?' I asked

her, hoping that she'd tell me how come Rob knew the whole story of what happened that night.

'I can't remember,' she said, pulling harshly at her hair. 'I, I think they might have, though. Do you want me to come with you to Shane's?'

'Why would I?' Did she think she could cover something up by being there with us?

'I think it would be best if I came too, just so you'll have an extra person there. Because it could be dangerous. Shane used to get violent before he left home, didn't he?'

'What was he like the night you saw him?'

She shuddered: 'I told you, Merle. I don't want to talk about it.'

Still the same line. It was darker now, with a sharper cold and rain. And the weather was beginning to have a physical effect on me. So we went home, saying we'd check whether Hannah was back and whether she'd go with us to see Shane tomorrow.

Ten

Who knows what Hannah felt when myself and Corinne arrived on her doorstep with Shane's address? The rain couldn't touch her from where she was standing in the doorway, but even though it continued to lash down on me and Corinne, anyone who had seen her face would have thought that Hannah was the worst off of the three of us. The darkness of her unlit hall and my words swept all over her. Who knows what she was thinking, what was going through her mind? She was obviously surprised to see Corinne, and she couldn't really say much in front of her, not knowing how much she had been told. Fair play to Hannah though, for letting me do the talking, letting me say that tomorrow would be perfect for looking Shane up, and that Corinne was insisting on coming along with us, just in case we needed her. She didn't even point out that tomorrow was Monday and we were both supposed to be in college. She just asked me what time I wanted to leave.

Her brother Shane. I rang Hannah, late that night when Corinne had been in bed for hours, even though I didn't know if Corinne was asleep or not. She never slept much. Most nights you'd hear her walking around, at three, four, five o'clock in the morning, and why should tonight be any different? She'd probably be worse than usual, if I was right about her and Shane. But Corinne was acting as if nothing had happened.

Hannah was quiet. So quiet that the last of the rain trickling softly against the windows was louder than her silence and the few words she did speak. I asked her if she minded about all this, was she pissed off with me? I wanted her to say something, anything to release the bottled-up pressure of the situation, even if what she said was as hostile as the cold damp air around the bottom stair I was sitting on. But she didn't react, so I just went on and told her about Saturday with Rob and Danielle.

She talked then. Oh, she was amazed, to say the least, and worried about her friend. In case Danielle was wondering who Shane was, Hannah asked me not to say anything to her about him until she had talked to her. On the surface, that was Hannah alright, trying to smooth and minimize everything as best she could. On the surface. Her words came easily and carelessly, as if she was just throwing them out to distract both herself and me from what was going to happen tomorrow. And I noticed that she didn't even speculate out loud about what could have made Rob act so strangely about Shane when she must have been wondering about it. I didn't say anything though. I was just so relieved that Hannah was coming tomorrow with no obstacles raised. There were no sharp remarks, no tension. No comments even about Corinne's insisting on coming with us in case something happened to us. Who knows what Hannah felt that night though, she didn't tell me.

Morning came. The rain had cleared overnight and left us with a clean blue sky. We set off in the muted light of the late autumn sun. Corinne was edgy, unsettling Hannah with her comments: 'It's weird, to be going to see Shane like this. I wonder what effect it'll have on you, Hannah. Last time I saw him, it made me realize the extent to which I couldn't connect emotionally with everything that happened around me.'

Hannah didn't answer her. She started walking faster, as if she thought that would help calm her down. But she walked reluctantly, as if she was afraid of getting where she was going. I watched her. She was a good bit ahead of us now, with a firm distance between us. I don't know why it came into my head, but it struck me that Hannah never walked ahead of anyone like this, even if there was no room on the path for her to walk beside the people she was with. When that happened, she'd walk in front of them alright, but she'd look back all the time, talking away, so there was never any distance between them.

We joined her in silence at the bus stop. Didn't have to wait long for a bus. Corinne sat beside me upstairs and Hannah sat in front of us, again. The air was hot, filthy stale and claustrophobic. I pulled at the window to try and get it open, but it was jammed. Corinne was clinging to the iron bar on the back of Hannah's seat as if she was trying to crush it. I genuinely thought she was going to break the bones of her hands, and was about to pull them away when Hannah spoke, shattering the sticky closeness with the weight of a new anxiety.

'I don't think of him as a brother, you know,' she said defensively. 'If I could cut myself off from him completely in my mind, I would. And I'd be all the better for it, instead of having him hanging over me all the time. And I don't care how bad that sounds, it's true.'

Especially when you were about to see a disturbing shadowy memory materialize into the here and now. What would her mam say if she knew? She'd probably tell Hannah not to go anywhere near him and that was probably what Hannah would like to hear. Only Hannah never told her much, especially about things like this. It was as if she was wary of her mam the way she was wary of their cat's claws. And that all went back to the trouble with Shane.

So what had he done to Corinne? I could see Hannah was afraid of that too. She used to look up to Corinne the same way I did, only nowhere near as much. Turning to Corinne, I saw that her hands were still crushing the bar. I pulled them off it, feeling even more displaced than I'd felt the other times her personality had seemed to crack in front of me.

We were in town now, and went to get another bus that would bring us out to where Shane lived. I was getting worried. What exactly was I going to do when we got there? Play it by ear? And what kind of state would the others be in? I could see Hannah getting more and more nervous throughout the ten minutes on this second bus. And I saw Corinne was getting more edgy, even though she was trying to appear calm: partly as if she didn't want us to know what she was thinking, and partly as if she was no longer resisting some terrible thing that she knew was going to happen.

We got off the bus. Went down two roads, and then turned on to the road that was meant to be Shane's, walking in the shadow of the big old trees you find only in old, rich areas. The fact that we were also walking in the shadow of Shane, Rob and Corinne made the trees oppressive for me, and their branches seemed to be closing in, pushing down on us, shutting out the sky.

'I wouldn't say many of these houses are in flats,' said Hannah, staring at the Mercs, the stone driveways and the perfect gardens.

We came to No. 6. Its heavy curtains and tie-backs dominated all three storeys of big, brooding windows, and it had a newly painted door with an expensive-looking night lantern and a heavy, old-fashioned door knocker. It may have looked kind of creepy, but it also looked as if it had had a lot of money spent on it.

'Merle, are you sure we're in the right place?' asked Hannah.

Oh yes, we were standing right in the oasis of Rob's blitzed landscape, unless there were two roads with the same name. I was unsettled by the disparity between the dive I'd expected and the elaborately cultivated house and garden I'd found. Then some guy came out the side door on to the bare lawn, wheeling a gleaming lawnmower.

'Ask him,' Corinne said when we saw he hadn't noticed us standing at the gate. She sounded angrily desperate to get this over and done with.

'Excuse me,' I said, opening the gate.

He didn't hear me so I walked right up to him. He was bent down with his back to me, fiddling with the machine.

'Excuse me,' I repeated.

He turned around and looked up, annoyed at the interruption.

'Are you *Shane*?' I asked.

It was the shock of a lifetime, staring at his face. He was still dead skinny-looking, but he appeared to be in seriously good shape, and the grey pallor and the wasted expression that I remembered were gone.

'I didn't recognize you, you've got a *tan*,' I said.

Hannah came running over to me, and Corinne followed, walking slowly. He stood up and stepped way back from the three of us who were staring in silence at his slicked-back blond hair and brand-new-looking jeans and shirt – imagine wearing new clothes for gardening, imagine new, expensive-looking clothes on *Shane*.

Hannah was squeezing my arm so hard I thought it was going to explode. 'I'm, I'm Hannah and this is Merle and Corinne, in case you don't recognize us,' she said, sounding like it was difficult for her to talk but she needed to.

Her brother looked uncomfortable. The same blond hair as Hannah, it was so obvious they were related. 'I recognized yis alright,' he said.

'Are you . . . are you . . .' Hannah's voice was shaky, her hand pressing my arm into serious pain. She was asking are you different now? How much different?

He was messing almost violently with the flex of the lawn-mower. 'Things are different for me now, I'm off drugs and I . . . I was on holidays for two weeks, I only got back on Saturday. That's where I got the tan.'

There was a silence. I wondered whether he was more frightening now in this forebodingly pseudo-normalized state than he had been before. Apart from the fact that I hadn't been expecting him to be like this, there was something lethal about his new state, as if the old Shane had just been pushed inside a cleaned-up shell and was simmering beneath the surface, on the verge of manifesting himself.

'Do you work here, then?' I asked, trying to make some sense of all this.

'I live here,' he said sharply, insulted.

'Are, are you just cutting the grass then?' Hannah was nearly crying, it was all too much for her. Cutting the grass – the grass that looked too cut.

'Yeah,' said Shane, softer, and nervous – he didn't know what to do either. 'It's a nice day out, especially after yesterday, so I thought I'd get it done before the winter comes and the real cold and wet sets in.'

'The place looks lovely,' said Corinne, as if she wanted to talk to him as well but didn't know what she wanted to say.

Shane scowled at her, started the lawnmower up and rammed it across a bit of the colourless grass as if he was trying to get rid of us. He stopped when he saw we were still there: 'So what do yis want?'

It was like a switch had gone off in him when Corinne had spoken. He hadn't been exactly welcoming before, but Corinne had turned him into downright ignorant. Hannah was dragging my arm away, but I stayed where I was, trying to orient myself back to where I was before seeing Shane swept the ground from under me.

'We just wanted to see how you were, after Corinne saw you in that pub a while back,' I said.

'What are you talking about, I haven't seen Corinne in years,' he said.

'She said I saw you, not that you saw me,' said Corinne in a strange, rhythmic pitch.

Both Hannah and myself looked at her in confused astonishment. But they must have met that night. Why else would he be so rude to her?

'I suppose you haven't seen Rob in years either,' I said.

'Fucking right I haven't,' he said.

'How does he know your address then?' I asked.

'Does he?' said Shane, pegging a stone at a blackbird that had landed on the wall beside him. 'Well how am I supposed to know how he got it? I hope he's not calling around as well, that's the last fucking thing I need.'

I watched the bird disappear into the oblivion of the sky, wishing we could do the same, wishing that an emotional mess hadn't entangled, trapped, and led us to this hostile garden. Hannah was crying.

'Come on, let's go,' she said.

Shane kicked the lawnmower back on, so I didn't have much choice. Just as we got to the gate, he stopped it again.

'Hannah!' he called over, embarrassed. She looked back. 'I'd, eh, I'd appreciate it if you didn't tell Mam or Dad or anyone anything about me or where I live.'

'I wasn't going to anyway,' she answered, wiping her eyes.

Once we were away from that house, all kinds of burning reactions set in, and we practically ran to the bus stop, trying to get away from him, and probably from ourselves as well. I was unsettled by what had happened. I was unsettled by myself for not knowing what to do, and by my sister. Corinne looked freaked out to me, and Hannah was crying the whole way home on the bus.

'I'm sorry about this,' said Hannah. 'I had no idea I was going to feel like this afterwards.'

'Don't worry about it,' said Corinne. 'That night in the pub, I was exactly like you are now. Seeing him made me feel serious physical self-disgust, and I, I hated myself. I wanted to die right there and then.'

Me and Hannah stared at her, unable to understand or empathize with her.

'I'm not like that at all,' sobbed Hannah. 'Or maybe I am a bit. I don't know, I mean, it's just, I spend my life hating my brother, so I don't think I'm going to feel any different when I see him today. But then when I do see him, it's a total shock, because the reasons for him being like that – the heroin, and, and, those awful friends I can't even remember properly – are gone. And he looks great. But he treats me like a stranger and that makes me feel real bad, because the reasons why he's a stranger are gone now, so I feel like it's all my fault.'

'Sure what could be your fault, Hannah?' I asked her.

'I don't know. I, I suppose that he, he probably feels there was no one there for him when he needed them. And anyway, why should he care about me, I never cared about him, sure I didn't even want to go looking for him!'

But she hadn't seen him since she was twelve, when she was too young to understand Shane's problems, never mind figure out where they came from. Right now I wished I knew where he'd gone wrong because that might give me some idea as to what had happened with Corinne, but this wasn't the time to go into that.

'I don't think his problem was you, Hannah,' I said, staring meaningfully at Corinne, who didn't seem to understand my implication. 'He was nicer to you than he was to us. He seemed to be mortified, though. I reckon he didn't know what to do. And besides, aren't you curious about what he's doing living in that big, posh gaff? He scrubs up well, doesn't he? Maybe the older bloke Corinne saw him with picked him up from the streets and cleaned up his act, so now he's ashamed of his past and wants to keep us all away. What do you reckon?'

'Merle!' said Corinne furiously. 'You didn't tell Hannah I reckoned her brother was on the game, did you?'

'What's the problem?' I asked, amazed at her intensity. Of course, she mightn't have wanted me telling Hannah. Oh well, it was too late for that now. 'Hannah's got a right to know about her brother,' I added. 'Anyway, he's hardly that if he's actually living there, cutting the grass with a state-of-the-art lawnmower. No, I reckon he's more of a toy boy, so it wouldn't do at all for him to have three young ones hanging around, now, would it?'

'I'm his sister, though,' she sobbed.

'Yeah Merle. Why are you making the whole thing out to be so sordid when there might be a less cynical explanation for everything?' Corinne was acting very insulted.

You're a fine one to talk, I thought, glaring at her. Maybe I am sensationalizing Shane – he could be as good as married for all I know – but maybe I'm sensationalizing him because that house reminds me of something. Something that would make anyone think sordid. This wasn't the time to bring it up. But it was the sort of thing that might inspire Corinne to talk, to explain the self-disgust she had felt that night when she saw Shane, tell us what had actually happened.

'Then why don't you find out what the story is with him, and let us all know if it's sordid or not,' I said to Corinne.

I was confused now, because if she had actually gone over to Shane that night, and if the bloke he was with was the owner of this house, then she'd have known that Shane wasn't on the game.

'Jesus, I'm staying well away from him,' she said, viciously.

She wouldn't be like this unless something had happened, would she? I mean, she couldn't have just seen him from the distance with this guy, assumed it was prostitution and freaked out because of it, could she?

'Promise me you won't do anything, Merle,' said Hannah. 'You saw what he was like. There's no point. Maybe one day I'll go back to him, when I've calmed down. I'd like to see him on my own, for myself, like, and I'll let you know how I get on. But don't you go doing anything without telling me.'

She stressed her words, making sure I understood that she was telling me not to go to him again looking for explanations about Corinne. Or about Rob for that matter. Not yet.

We were outside Hannah's house. I shivered in the darkening cold. Their hall light was on, a cold yellow that shone through the brown curvy glass window and the infamous bars, and turned the texture of the door into that of fancy whiskey bottles. We said goodbye, for now.

Eleven

Serious physical self-disgust, Corinne had said. She had felt serious physical self-disgust when she saw Shane that night. Well, I had my own story about serious physical self-disgust, a story that had pushed itself to the front of my mind when I saw Shane's house. That was what had made me think sordid. The more I thought about it, the more I reckoned I should talk to Corinne about it, much as I didn't want to. Because the more I thought about it, the more I reckoned that this particular story would make her say *something*, even if she didn't mean to say it, and what she said might explain something about her and Shane.

The story goes like this. Six years ago, me and Corinne were being left at home while Mam went away, and Mam didn't know what to do about me. She knew that Corinne would look after me if she was asked to. But still, Mam worried. Corinne liked to go out a lot, and I couldn't be left on my own in the house at night because I was only twelve.

'Go on,' said Corinne. 'We'll be OK here on our own. It's only for a weekend. And besides, if I do want to go out some night, I'll just send Merle across the road to spend the night with Hannah.'

'I don't know, girls. It might be better if someone was staying here,' said Mam.

'But the only one you can get is our bleeding great-aunt Eileen, and you can't do that to us Mam, you can't,' I said.

'Yeah Mam. It's summer, and we won't be able to do anything if she's here,' said Corinne. 'She'll make a right show of us, dragging us up to Mass on Sunday morning and stuff. And the state of her! I mean, for fuck sake.'

'You watch your mouth, young one. And there's plenty your age who go to Mass every Sunday. I let you two get away with murder.'

'But she embarrasses the life out of us, Mam,' Corinne said. 'I'll be in the sitting room watching telly with my friends, and the next thing it'll be six o clock and she'll come in, put on RTE1 for the news, and expect me to say the fucking angelus with her when it comes on.'

'And remember what happened last time,' I said.

Corinne had said she didn't know any prayers and walked out of the room, leaving her friends sitting there, wondering what to do. Eileen had been shocked and horrified, and Mam had a lot of trouble sorting that one out.

'She doesn't even like us, Mam,' said Corinne. 'We can tell.'

So the two of us got left on our own.

Ever since the year before, Corinne had had a lot of time for me. She seemed to prefer talking to me than to her friends. I could understand that alright, because even then, she had very bad taste in friends. These ones were harmless enough. It's just that they were obsessed with the finer details of what other people thought of them, what their boyfriends had said about them to the other fellas, all this kind of stuff. I used to listen to them talk, when they were getting ready in Corinne's room to go out. First they'd want to wear slutty tops and little skirts because they thought they looked cool, and then they'd worry themselves sick because they thought they looked like tarts.

Even Corinne slagged them to me. She said she could talk to

me, because I didn't give a shit about anything, she could see that I'd always do exactly what I wanted to, and she liked that. She'd met a few girls lately who were like that. They hung out with these really cool bands in town. She told me they were all amazing, but I hadn't actually met any of these people yet.

On Friday night, it was just some of her old friends that came over. I was in the sitting room, knocking back cans of beer with them. They were saying things like: 'Do you not mind your little sister drinking like that?', 'Can she hold her drink?', 'Fucking hell'. Corinne was changing, getting more detached. I could see her doing all the right stuff and talking to people, and so on. But her heart wasn't really in it anymore.

Her best friend, Niamh, had this habit of going off with some fella and his friends for a month or so in the summer and hanging around with them instead of Corinne. Then she'd come back to Corinne, when she'd broken it off with the fella and couldn't hang around with them anymore. Corinne didn't seem to mind much about that. But it could annoy her sometimes, like tonight, when Niamh and her latest boyfriend came around for the first time in weeks, just because Corinne had a free gaff. They went and sat in the kitchen and didn't talk to anyone all night, not even Corinne, which really got to her.

'For fuck sake,' she said to me in private. 'They're in there snogging now. Go in and tell her I'll kill her if they go near the bedrooms. If she wants to shag him they can at least go out into the garden.'

I went into the kitchen and did that. I was thinking 'the cheek of that Niamh one, using Corinne like this'. And I could see they were thinking 'the cheek of Corinne, sending her sister in like that. Who the fuck do they think they are?'

I felt protective and protected. Corinne wasn't even trying to control her restlessness anymore. I could see it written all over her, in the way she looked at the house, and in the almost desperate way she drank and smoked – early in the night, she drank a lot very fast, and then she stopped drinking altogether, as if it was no longer working for her.

Eventually, everybody left and she stayed up the rest of the night with me. We lay on the sitting room floor, listening to music, with the curtains opened to let in the night-time sky. That was the best part of the night for both of us. And I was still awake when the dawn came, which was a great feeling.

I must have gone upstairs at some stage and fallen asleep, because I woke up in my own bed the following afternoon. When I went downstairs, I saw that the place had been all cleaned up. Corinne was sitting on the kitchen table beside a full black sack.

'I don't know what I'm going to do with you tonight,' she said. 'Because I'm going out, and Hannah isn't home – someone told me that her and her parents went off to the beach and won't be back until late.'

'Where are you going?' I asked her. She sounded very excited.

'I'm going to this guy's party – he's a friend of Hilary, only you don't know Hilary, do you? Anyway, he's in a band and his parents have this amazing, big house somewhere, and he's having a party there tonight.'

From the way Corinne was talking, I could tell that it was going to be some night.

'Would I be too young to go?' I asked. I was desperate to go, but I reckoned there was no way she could bring me to something like that.

'I'd say so, yeah,' she said, looking at me sympathetically. But her mind was really on how she was going to offload me. 'Is there no one else you could stay with? What about your other friends?' she asked.

'Mam says I'm not to stay with anyone except Hannah,' I reminded her.

Corinne looked disappointed. And I was wanting more and more to go to this party.

'Are you sure I can't go?' I pushed. 'I could talk to them all about music. And I could tell them that Mam's going to get me a real electric guitar for Christmas, if she has the money.'

'Oh Merle,' she said, laughing. 'You're something else, do you know that. Sometimes you come across as being a lot older than you are, and sometimes a lot younger.'

I was upset. 'Well, I could just sit in a corner then, and drink. I'd be happy enough just to look on at everything.'

She was touched. 'Oh you poor little love. I'm not trying to get at you. It's just that these fellas, well they can be real bastards very easily – they have such big heads, and they don't give a fuck about anyone else's feelings. So I don't know how well they'd react to you saying something like that about getting a guitar.'

'Why do you want to go then?' I asked defensively.

That threw her a bit, made her kind of confused and hesitant. 'Well you know, things are never that simple,' she said with authority but without knowing what point she was trying to make. 'No, fuck it. If you don't go, I can't go. And anyway, you get on very well with my normal friends, so why shouldn't you be the same with these ones? And besides, you look old for your age, and I'll keep an eye on you,' she said, reassuring herself that nothing would go wrong, though I didn't see what she could be afraid of, apart from the fact that I might be a bit young for this. 'OK, that's it. You're going,' she said.

Corinne was so hyper that day. The sun was shining, and we could sunbathe out the back with music on and run around the place shouting, knowing there was no one in the house to hear us. We could eat whatever we wanted whenever we wanted it, which was great, because we had to go out real early to make it worth our while going out at all – we would have to leave this party early tonight if we wanted to catch our buses home.

I don't remember paying much attention to Corinne's new friend Hilary on the bus out, and I don't know why that was, because I'd been looking forward to meeting her. Maybe it was because Corinne and Hilary were sitting in front of me and I got distracted from them, looking out the window. I can still see the bus, the bright evening sky, the traffic lights and the roads more clearly than I can see Hilary. But for some reason, I can hear her voice, which was loud and sharp.

The party was in a big old house that looked just like Shane's from the outside. It was kind of pretentious, though – overdone and with a lot of big dark furniture. Corinne whispered to me that this fella's parents were meant to be really rich, but even though she sounded impressed, I don't think she liked the house much either. Nothing in it seemed to be real, including the people. Maybe this was because they all looked like something out of a magazine rather than like people and a place that really existed.

I was a bit disoriented from having been suddenly thrown into a different environment. Everyone was nice to me, but in a disconnected way, as if they weren't really talking to me, as if I was insignificant, but that they thought it was only right that I should want to be there with them. Someone started singing a song I knew with someone else playing guitar to it, and hearing that familiar music in this place made me feel uncomfortable for some reason. I just didn't feel right there, and I didn't know why.

Corinne was pulled out of the room to go talk to a girl who was upset about something. I sat in a corner, watching everything that was going on, thinking that if Hannah was here we'd at least have a laugh, watching all the fellas that were in bands and the girls that were with them. Something stopped me from wanting to talk to these people. I suppose it was because I felt like an outsider. So I went looking for Corinne, but I couldn't find her. Eventually, I wandered into the room next to the one I had been in, and when I saw that there was nobody in there, I decided I'd wait there for a while.

I go and sit in an armchair beside the fireplace. Then this fella comes in and sits on the floor in front of me. He's very good-looking and he knows it. He loves himself. And he's very image-conscious, very carefully dressed. He knows who I am. I think I was introduced to him earlier, but I'm not sure, because there's several other fellas that look quite like him – same hair, same clothes. He's sitting on the floor in front of me, and I don't like it. I don't like his eyes.

'How do I seem to you?' he asks me.

What kind of a question is that, I wonder.

'In what way?' I ask him.

'In what way, in what way,' he repeats to himself scornfully. 'For fuck sake. In what way do you think?'

Just say nothing, I tell myself. I don't know what the story is here. He's getting a thrill out of something. I can see it in his eyes. I'm out of my depth here, and I don't know what to do. There's a very strange look in his eyes. It has me glued to my chair and it's making me feel uneasy.

'Why don't you talk to me? You *can* talk, can't you?' he asks.

I tell myself again to say nothing.

'Your sister says you want to be in a band. Is that true?' he asks in the same threatening tone of voice.

I don't answer him. He wants to make me feel stupid, but I'm not going to let him.

'Oh come on,' he says. 'It's not enough to just look good, you know. You have to be able to talk as well.'

'Of course I can talk,' I say, wondering why I'm not able to get up and leave the room. Why am I letting myself be so frightened by his eyes and his voice?

'Glad to hear it,' he says. 'And of course, you do look good. What do you think of me? Do I look good?'

Now I'm back to not being able to say anything. Where is Corinne? I'm angry with her for leaving me alone, and I wish I had never asked her to bring me here. He's looking me up and down now, really giving me the creeps.

'How old did your sister say you were? Twelve?' he asks. 'Usually that would be way too young for me, but in your case, I'll make an exception.'

He's standing over me now, leaning on the mantelpiece and looking down at me. This is getting very embarrassing. I can't move with the tension, and my chair feels like it's on fire.

'I'm not interested,' is all I can manage to say.

He's annoyed and angry with me now. 'Are you turning me down?' he asks. From the way he's looking at me, I think he's going to hit me, but instead, he says: 'I don't think I can let you do that.' He pulls me down on to the floor, and I try to fight him off. I think I'm going to explode with fear and pain and horror, but before my panicked head can tell me to scream, I hear the door open and something smashing.

The noise has broken the situation. He gets off me and leaves the room. I look up and see that Corinne has just thrown a big vase across the floor. It was her. She broke this up. Her friend Hilary is standing in the door, looking completely stunned. Corinne comes over and takes me out of the room. She screams and shakes. I feel like I've been buried in a pile of ice, so I can't feel anything or talk to her, I can only watch.

Corinne runs out the front door and I follow. She pulls the door behind her without locking it, and we sit on the step. Her friend Hilary comes out after us.

'Did he just jump on you or were you leading him on?' Hilary asks me.

Corinne is crying now, scraping her face over and over. 'Did you not see her trying to fight him off?' Corinne shouts at Hilary. I can see Corinne's face bleeding. Each trickle of blood seems to melt a bit of the ice that surrounds me, so I feel as if it's my face, because I'm going to slash my own face as soon as I can move again.

Hilary puts her arm around Corinne and says not to worry, that it wasn't her fault. She tells us that he was in a weird mood tonight anyway – his band had thought they were getting a record deal, but it fell through, so they were all a bit dodgy tonight, especially him. I'm still frightened, and I feel strange. Everything around me seems to be happening in slow motion. Even the darkening sky seems to be so bright that I'm almost blinded by it.

'Why did you throw that vase,' Hilary asks, laughing self-consciously and trying to take Corinne's hands away from her face. 'It must have cost a fucking fortune. You could have just said something to him, you know.' Corinne doesn't answer her, but Hilary can't manage to get Corinne's hands down. 'Are you alright,' Hilary asks me. 'It's not that big a deal really, even though you're still only a kid. But he wouldn't have done anything to you if you'd told him not to.'

You could have done something, you could have said something, I hear myself thinking. All the ice is gone now. I put my fingers in my mouth and try to bite them off as hard as I can. Corinne's hand comes away from her face and takes my fingers out of my mouth.

'We'd better go home now,' says Corinne.

We're both crying hysterically now. We walk to the bus stop. Even the street lights hurt my eyes.

'What the fuck are you doing with them fellas?' I ask Corinne as soon as we're on the bus. But even though she's still distraught, I can see that she's defensive and that she's trying to think up an excuse for them. And that makes me feel really sick, more so than anything else ever could.

'I haven't seen that before. It never happened to me before,' she whispers.

'It didn't happen to you, it happened to me!' I scream. The other two people on the bus look around at us and Corinne puts her hand over my mouth. As soon as she touches me, she starts shaking.

'It might as well have happened to me, I feel like it did. Oh God. The one night I bring you out, you fuck everything up, you fuck both of us up!'

As soon as I hear that, I feel serious physical self-disgust. My hands go to my face. I want to scrape and burn every inch of my skin off so that I can kill the person this happened to.

'I can't be the only one things happened to at that party. I can't be,' I insist. 'What was wrong with the girl you had to go and see, leaving me on my own?'

'Normal things,' Corinne answers angrily.

'What?'

'Just some normal thing about some fella.'

'Are you saying there's something wrong with me?' I ask, horrified.

'No. You're just too young,' says Corinne, still crying. She's scraping her face as well.

'But I didn't do anything!'

She knows that, doesn't she? She just wants it to be my fault so that she doesn't have to feel guilty about hanging around with that crowd in the future.

'I don't know what the story is, Merle. I really don't,' she says. And as far as she's concerned, that's the end of it.

But there's one more thing I want to say to her: 'Look what time it is. If we hadn't left then, we'd have missed our bus, and we'd have had to spend the night there! And what would have happened to me if I'd been there all night?'

But when I was at home in my bed that night, it was the

thought of Corinne that frightened me more than the thought of your man. She was puking her guts up all night. Even I didn't puke up. I lay there the whole night, listening to Corinne going in and out of the bathroom and feeling guilty for having made her bring me to the party and for having done this to her.

For a long time afterwards, I wanted to burn myself. But time passed. And eventually, I managed to block it out completely, even though I remained afraid of anything like that ever happening again. The worse thing about it was that it had made me frightened of my sister's world. That party and the other bad night I spent with her friends, two years later, really pulled me and Corinne apart. I tried not to let it drive me away, and I pretended to myself that it hadn't, but deep down, I knew that it had. Maybe that was why I needed so much to believe that there was some concrete explanation for why Corinne wanted to kill herself. It was as if uncovering that reason would make up for what had happened and for the cold, detached way I had reacted the night she tried to die.

In any case, I was going to talk to Corinne about the party for the first time since that night all those years ago.

Twelve

It was the following night. I was lying on the bed in Corinne's room, looking at the window. The curtains were closed but there was a gap between them at the top, so I could see the night, and the build-up of condensation on the glass. I suddenly felt chill, even though the heating was on, and put my head down on the bed. When I looked up, she was putting on her make-up to go out with Mam later on, and I watched her. Corinne's hand was steady to the point of stiffness, and there would have been something violent about it if the movements hadn't been so slow. The room was stuffy, making me feel numb and half-asleep, but Corinne's heaviness was caused by something beyond this room. I jumped up, wanting to shake off the room. She flinched at the sound and looked around.

'Shane wasn't very happy to see us, was he?' I said.

She rolled her eyes, but the movement was exaggerated and awkward. 'That's to be expected, I suppose,' she said.

'Why's that?' I asked.

'Well, like you said yourself, he's probably trying to build a new life for himself away from the past.'

Which past? These last six years that we knew nothing about, or all the time he had spent growing up here on this road, with Hannah and her cold, quiet parents?

'What went wrong with Shane, anyway? Me and Hannah were too young to know,' I asked Corinne.

I was thinking at the same time that I'd never known why she hated it here so much more than I did. I always assumed that Corinne just felt the same about these claustrophobic time-stained grey houses as I did. And I also imagined that she had the same sense of imbalance when the sky shone dazzling, transforming everything with shades of endless colour and possibility – everything except the houses, which reacted under its gaze by crumpling into even more dirty-grey dinginess. Only I thought Corinne must have felt it more deeply, the way when I was a small kid I thought she was much more of everything than I was, and that, if I tried hard enough, I'd be just like her when I got to be her age. Only she was always four years ahead of me, and the older she got, the more my aspiration deteriorated into hurt and confusion, mainly thanks to the two bad nights with her friends. But even still, I never stopped identifying with her.

'I didn't know Shane well at all,' said Corinne.

'Oh,' I said, feeling a sense of loss, a confirmation of a wall having gone up between us. I'll continue though – anything not to let that distance push me away. 'I thought you'd have known him well, seeing as you were the same age and living just across the road from each other.'

'Well, I didn't,' said Corinne.

'Obviously not,' I said. 'Because you told me that him and Rob were friends. Did you see the way he reacted when I said Rob knew where he lived?'

'Yeah, that was the only good thing about the whole encounter. Like I said before, I can't stand Rob. As a matter of fact, I hate him with a passion. At least you haven't been to see him lately – I did that much for you by coming back.'

Corinne said that with a chill that would have overpowered the heating if I hadn't been cold already. Rob gave her the creeps, she'd said. I can understand that, he gives me them too, after the way he acted about Shane's address . . . I got that map on Saturday night, and it's only Tuesday now, I thought, though Saturday seems years ago already when I try to relate it to all that's happened since. I wondered if Corinne ever experienced anything with him like I had. Rob can't have just done all that with the map out of spite. There's more to it, there has to be. But then I wondered if I only wanted Rob to have a secret reason for concealing it and a connection with Shane so that I could justify his actions, so that I could redeem him in my mind as a figure of depth. And it was also likely that I only wanted Corinne to have had a similar relationship with him so that I could explain her actions. All of this combined with my tension to make me lose my balance. The four walls seemed to sway and shake as I tried to focus my mind on what I meant to talk about.

'That house Shane's living in reminded me of something,' I said.

The torn corner of a red cushion on the floor caught my eye. A combination of the bright colour and the exploded material burnt away at my eyes.

'Yeah? Of course, what am I saying, I'm not exactly mad about Shane either,' Corinne said, as if she'd only heard my voice and not what I'd said.

She was practically pulling her hair off her head, trying to put it up in the little mirror.

'Here, I'll do that for you,' I said. 'The little mirror's no good for that.'

Soon after Corinne had left here for the first time, the big mirror had been broken when everything from Mam's room got put into this room while Mam's room was being done up. Mam kept saying for a while afterwards that she must get a new mirror, but because Corinne wasn't here there was no real need for it, so she didn't. And when Corinne came back for Christmas that year and saw the mirror gone, she sat on the bed, staring at the empty space, and told me that was when it hit her that she was really gone for good. I don't know whether she thought that was good or bad – it was a bit of both, I suppose – but the missing mirror had something of an impact on her alright. And then, the next time she came home was the time she tried to kill herself. So I wanted things to work out this time around, because otherwise I'd start thinking it was bad luck for her to come home.

Corinne sat completely still, not even moving when I pulled hard with the hairbrush, which I did twice to see if I could make her react to it. I took my time, trying to figure my voice back to where it was.

'You know what Shane's house reminds me of?' I said, smoothly clipping her hair up. 'That house you brought me to when I was twelve.'

She only half-looked at me, her glance thorough but unfocused.

'You know,' I said. 'The house where that party was, where there was that fella.'

She turned to me. In her voice I heard her mind and understood that it was something to frighten both of us. 'How could I ever forget,' she said, all spaced-out. 'I come into the room, and there you are. God, I don't know how you could stand the pain of it – him on top of you, smothering you into that hard pointy chair.'

The mist of her voice was flickering into suffocating, burning, treacherous smoke. I stared at her, lost and confused.

'And the jewellery,' she said, 'how can you stand all that heavy jewellery he's given you, strangling your neck and digging into your skin?'

'Stop!' I screamed. 'You're remembering it wrong!'

She backed into the corner and stared at me suspiciously. 'How could I ever forget,' she whispered.

'I, I never thought you would!' I said, shaking. 'The way you reacted that night, you'd think it had happened to *you*. But it obviously wasn't important enough for you to remember it right, was it?'

She looked at me in shock. 'Back in a minute,' she whispered.

I heard the door opening. It was such a sordid and ominous sound, and I wanted to be able to pull her back into the room and make her talk, explain to me why she forgot. Make her tell me that no, her forgetting has nothing to do with me, it happened because, because her brain is confused and she's a mess. But I didn't know how, and I let her go. The door closed, locking me further into this splintered world of ours. I heard her in the bathroom, she was puking her guts up. You see, she *is* a mess, her brain *is* confused. She's not being bad to me. She didn't remember wrong because she doesn't care about me, did she?

I went into my own room, lay down on the bed, head down so I couldn't see. Then I grasped the covers so tightly with my fists that I couldn't feel them or the room anymore.

Her brain is confused. She's been fucked up ever since she saw Shane in a pub and tried to kill herself. She may have messed up the details of that party, but remember what happened on Sunday afternoon? She freaked out when that oul drunk wanted a smoke, and she ran up that dodgy lane, saying he had a grey jumper on. A grey jumper? I'm going to find out what happened that night with Shane if it's the last thing I do.

But remember, remember the party itself. Remember what she said afterwards, when she was all hysterical: 'That never happened to me before,' she said. 'Happened to me?' It didn't happen to her, it happened to me. Her brain must have been confused even then. Not that I picked up on it, being all freaked out myself. I thought she was just saying that because she was freaked out too. 'It didn't happen to you, it happened to me,' was all I could manage to say back to her. That detail had lodged itself in my mind, but I hadn't thought about it much.

So what am I saying then? If her brain gets confused every time she sees or thinks about a traumatic incident, making her mind blur and distort the images belonging to that incident, then something terrible must have happened to her. It makes sense doesn't it, seeing as she's all fucked up? And what if, what if, instead of something happening that night with Shane, some-thing had happened between them years ago. Because that party was six years ago, when she was sixteen. And Shane left home when he was sixteen, after smashing the place up. In fact, all his problems might have been caused by whatever had happened. That would make sense, wouldn't it? And then, when Corinne saw Shane in that pub, she would have been reminded of whatever awful thing had happened. They might even have talked about it. One way or another, he would have re-awoken her memories of the trauma, and that would have made her want to die.

There's one problem, though. If this thing's so terrible that remembering it made her want to die, then why didn't she kill herself at sixteen, when it happened? That would have been the time to do it. And besides, from what Rob said, something must have happened with Shane in the pub that night. Because he said 'I'm surprised she told you about that,' didn't he?

But still, though. Maybe two things happened: one when they were sixteen and one six years later, when Shane and Corinne met again. These two things could have been related, and the second one could have been the final straw for Corinne.

What's the story with that drunk, anyway? Corinne saw him, freaked out, and ran up the lane. Then she told me that she needed to confront that lane and all the things that used to frighten her in order to see them differently. But why would she associate him with terror? For God's sake, he only asked me for a smoke. So why would she pick the whole situation up so inaccurately? She's always getting details wrong. It's as if she's living in some other world. I suppose that whatever happened with her and Shane messed up her mind so much that every little incident seems to her to be traumatic. What is it, though? All I can guess is that something terrible had happened twice.

So how am I going to find out what it is? For a start, who else even knows about it? Rob, of course. Because why else would Corinne hate him so much? She even came home specially to make sure I stayed away from him. In fact, he must have played a very dodgy part in whatever happened, because why else would Corinne hate him and not Shane? And he must be ashamed of it too, because why else would he have refused to tell me what had happened and then lie to me about not knowing where Shane lives? Bastard.

Of course Rob's involved. He has guilt written all over him. Will I ever forget that map? That blacked-out city on a page that had been folded into oblivion and hidden in a guitar. And look what he'd done to all the other maps: they'd been ripped out of the book and thrown in the grate, all ready to be burnt. The fucking gobshite.

And what about that bus ticket? What's that all about – him keeping a bus ticket for over a month and then saying he never took the bus anywhere. Jesus Christ! I have that ticket, don't I? Yes, because I remember picking it up from the floor where Danielle had thrown it, looking at it and not recognizing the stop. And then I think I automatically put it in my jacket pocket!

I took down my jacket from the back of the door and emptied the pockets, wondering if I still had it. It was there alright, and this time I recognised the stop: Shane's.

So what's going on, then? Well, I know that the ticket's a month old and that Rob's been acting weird for a month, according to Danielle – that's why she thought he was doing the dirt. And it's a month since Corinne tried to kill herself.

I looked at the date on the ticket. Rob had gone there the night after Corinne tried to kill herself.

But Shane acted as if Rob hadn't been to the house. He was actually pretty angry that Rob knew where he lived. So what's the story then? Is Shane lying too? Unless Rob had just stalked the gaff instead of calling at the door. That'd be it alright. For some strange reason, Corinne might have told Rob what happened with Shane in the pub, even though I had thought originally that she couldn't have been talking to him around the time. Rob might have known where Shane lived and then, because he was guilty of something, and because talking to Corinne had brought it all back, he might have gone over there, wanting to see Shane, but too afraid to call in to him.

Well, who am I going to get to tell me? Corinne won't. That's understandable. It's obviously something so bad that it's too difficult for her to talk about. Maybe she's even afraid of what I'd think. It must be bad then, because she spent the whole of Sunday telling me how messed up she feels but not telling me why. And Shane isn't likely to tell me either – especially now that he has a new life. And anyway, Hannah asked me not to go near him again. Of course I won't, seeing as she got so upset yesterday after talking to him.

That just leaves Rob the bastard, then. I do not want to see him. It makes me sick to think that I spent a whole summer hanging around him without knowing that he had done something to my sister. And to think I was mad about him and everything! Oh God. It gives me the creeps.

But there's no way out of it. I have to go and ask Rob about all this. I have to. I know he lied to me before, but this time will be different. I'll confront him, saying I know all about it, I know exactly what he did, and hopefully I'll catch him out that way.

Even if he denies it, he'll have to tell me what it is he's denying, and that's how I'll find out what happened. So it'll be worth it. No matter how bad I feel about going to see him, it'll be worth it.

Thirteen

That night was one of very bad dreams. Burnt-out moons and blighted landscapes and disfigured faces that dissolved into nothingness before I could reach them. As I stood in the middle of it all, I got this strange, frightening feeling that my sister should be there too, but I couldn't remember why, no matter how hard I tried. What else could I expect? That's what I get for thinking and talking about that party – I've been trying to forget about it since I was twelve. Still, it could be worse. At least I haven't been talking about what happened when I was fourteen.

I put off going to see Rob until Saturday, when I wasn't working. I got up early enough that day. Surprisingly, Corinne was already out. She'd told Mam that she was going into town to see a few people and do a few things. Mam thought this was great, Corinne bouncing around the place. The way Mam talked, you'd think Corinne was a baby.

'She's looking much better these days, isn't she?' Mam asked.

'Oh she is, yeah,' I said, not liking to comment that Corinne always looked well, it meant absolutely nothing.

It's a clear bright day, and I want to be out too. It's bitterly cold, maybe cold enough to freeze and calm someone like me, someone who feels they've been blasted into radioactive, incohesive fragments. It's too cold for other people to go out for the sake of being outside. It's only nice dry weather for them if they have to go somewhere. But I'm going somewhere. I'm going to see Rob. Only I don't want to see him, I just want to go out for the sake of being outside. Away from Corinne. And away from Rob.

Oh God. Rob. At least I can do this, at least I'm doing it. Let's just hope I have what it takes to get the answers I need.

Where is Corinne today, anyway? You don't really think she's out shopping and having coffee, do you? Oh well, I suppose that's another story, one I'll find out about later.

It's so good to be out of that house, walking away from it, watching the clouds of my breath and cigarette smoke and the clear blue sky. I'm even happy that the bus is crowded, because for some reason, I know that if I had gotten a seat, I would have unfrozen and fallen to pieces again. I just want to stand and walk.

Once I got off the bus, I stood still for a minute, thinking how the walk to where Rob lives is five, maybe ten minutes long. In that time, I'll be there, on the doorstep of that encapsulated, smoke-drenched corner of the world that never changes except to deteriorate slowly but surely. But I'm not worried about that right now. I'm just so relieved to be doing this, so almost hysterically glad that I've turned the negative implications of Corinne forgetting what happened at the party into a constructive explanation that could help me resolve everything.

Danielle was in the house. I saw her when I pushed in the front door. She was in the dark hallway, hanging up the phone. She looked at me, I was the last person she expected to see and she didn't know what to say to me. I didn't say anything because I was adjusting to being inside, being in this inside with these people. And the relief I'd felt outside was gone. The tension and the not wanting to do this was back. Then Danielle said how she hadn't seen me in ages, hadn't seen me around college.

'That's right, yeah,' I said. 'I've been, you know, busy.'

She nodded and said 'oh right' or something like that. She was still standing there, looking at me, not knowing what to say, thinking how the last time she saw me was last Saturday night when she was fighting with Rob. So I talked and talked to her, told her how great it was to see her again. For some reason, I got very hyper – I suppose it was a distorted expression of the high-pitched tension I was feeling – and Danielle started smiling, which was good, because it meant the awkwardness was gone.

'Come on, we have to see Rob,' I said, walking up the stairs. Then I stopped and turned around, so suddenly I banged into her and nearly sent her flying back down. 'You are still talking to each other and going out and all?'

She laughed. 'Yes. So there's no need to push me down the stairs.'

Good. I hadn't put my foot in it. I was on such a high now that I wouldn't have known what to say to her if I had. Yes, on a high, because ... because in ten more minutes, I'm going to have all the answers I need. So I think positive and try to push all the tension away.

I knocked on the door and opened it. But what did we find? Oh Corinne, I knew you had your derangements, but this? What the fuck are you doing here, locked senseless, sitting on the couch beside Rob with the remains of quite a little party lying around the room? I picked up an empty bottle of vodka and saw that it was bought in our local offo. Did you pay for all this? You must have planned it all in advance, carried all that drink all the way over here. Why?

Standing there, I watched my plans and momentum dissolve and flow away. I stared over at the two of them sitting together. No way does it look like Corinne hates him or like he's full of guilt from something he did to her. No. In fact, they look like two of a kind, with the dark hair and ghostly skinniness. So good-looking. So full of a shared, exclusive, darkened mystique. She looks more like his sister than mine, only that's not the impression of the situation that would spring to mind. Not to Danielle's mind, anyway. She was looking at Corinne, angry and confused, all those suspicions of Rob doing the dirt coming back into her face.

'What are you doing here, Corinne?' I asked, a world of loneliness and disillusionment enveloping me.

She doesn't even seem to realize that I've just spoken. She looks calm and melancholy. And she looks really pissed. So does he, only he looks horrified that his girlfriend is standing at the door. Danielle's staring at me now. I can feel the weight of all the suspicions that have risen up in her, and they're bloody heavy.

'Oh, I just felt like coming over,' Corinne said, changing her position on the couch, picking up an empty beer can that was in her way and throwing it on the floor. She still hasn't reacted mentally to the implications of my finding her here.

'Is she a friend of yours?' Danielle asked me.

'She's my sister,' I answered slowly, even though I'm almost not sure she is anymore.

Danielle gave me one venomous look of disgust, long and slow, before going over to stand in front of them.

'I didn't know you had a sister who knew Rob so well,' she said.

'Neither did I,' I said, wanting to sound angry but too shocked to do so.

Danielle took this as implying that Corinne was the secret 'other girlfriend'. 'So how long have you known Rob?' she asked Corinne.

'How long have *you* known Rob?' Corinne answered. Then a look of confusion passed over her face as she realized who she was talking to. 'Are you his girlfriend?' she asked. 'No way. I've been thinking about you, wondering what you looked like, and here you are!'

116

Danielle looked at Rob. He stared back at her, confused, but he didn't say anything, so she stormed out. Went down the stairs, walking a few steps then running. I strained my ears and heard the door of her flat close quietly behind her.

A few loaded minutes of inaction passed. I focused my energies on watching the inhabitants of this new, alienating world, wondering what to do. Rob got up, like he half-wanted to go after Danielle. But he was flustered and couldn't bring himself to go. His anger had to go somewhere though, so he shouted at Corinne: 'Get the fuck out, go on.' She laughed, but strangely, as if she wasn't sure.

'It's not funny,' I said.

'What are you looking at me for,' she said, still laughing.

'I don't know,' I said. 'It might have something to do with the fact that you told me you came home because you hate Rob so much you want to keep me away from him.'

'Well it didn't work, did it? Because if it did, you wouldn't be here,' she said. But she wasn't laughing anymore. She looked a bit disturbed and confused, as if she didn't know why she should be disturbed and was trying to suppress it.

'But you didn't know I was coming, did you? And it's not like I wanted to come, either. I can't stand the sight of Rob since Saturday night, when I found out he lied to me about Shane's address,' I told her, trying to establish a logical connection between all this and all that had gone before it.

I stared at Rob. He tried to say something, but not a word came out, only a mumble. But the sound caught Corinne's attention, and she looked at him warily, as if afraid of what he wanted to tell me. He turned away from her and stayed looking at me. So I walked towards him, thinking that he had something important to say to me, thinking that if I'm closer I'll make more of an impression on him when I tell him I know why he hid Shane's address, even though I'll only be pretending. But how can I lie convincingly now that Corinne's here and my picture of the connection between the three of them has been smashed?

'I saw Shane one night in town,' said Rob slowly. 'I saw him, and without knowing why, I followed him. He didn't see me. I got on his bus and he still didn't see me. So I was able to follow him all the way home, and stand outside for a long, long time, staring at his windows.'

As he spoke, a heavy smoke shadow seemed to materialize and hang over him, and for a moment after he fell silent, it expanded to include Corinne. It shut me out so completely that I didn't think to question him for a few seconds. Until, angry with myself and upset about Corinne, I took a step forward so that I could be standing right in front of him when I asked him why he didn't just go up and talk to Shane and why Corinne said she didn't either. But I was so stressed out that I forgot about the loose floorboard underneath the carpet beside the couch. So I walked right over that floorboard, and when it gave way beneath the carpet, I tripped, knocking over the table and everything on it. Lying on the floor, I realized that I'd cut myself on broken glass. I looked up at Rob, and was surprised to see that he looked pleased. He doesn't even ask if I'm alright. Neither does she. In fact, she looks as if she didn't even see it happen, like I'm not even in the room, even though I'm right in front of her. And I don't know what to do with them. I don't know what I can do. I don't even know if I should do anything.

It wasn't a very deep cut, but it was messy. I washed it in Rob's full-up sink and got whatever tissues I had. I looked in Corinne's jacket and saw that she had about half a box of tissues with her and all her make-up. I opened her compact and decided to use the sponge because it wouldn't disintegrate. I pressed its clean side into my hand, hoping to stop the bleeding. They were both still just sitting there, him watching me closely. He's a prick. In a rush of anger, I threw the blood-soaked sponge at him.

Unfortunately, I missed. Then I threw Corinne's jacket at her. She looked up and put it on.

'Are we going now?' she asked indifferently.

'That's not why I threw your jacket at you, no,' I answered, wondering what kind of a headcase she was. I didn't see it as a reasonable question, not in a situation like this.

'What did you do it for, then?' she asked.

'I don't know. Because, because I'm majorly pissed off. Why do you think?'

She didn't answer me and I felt kind of lost. So I made a last appeal, more for the sake of myself and my displaced feelings than for anything else, because I didn't really think I was going to get anything out of them.

'Are, are either of you going to tell me what the story is with yourselves and Shane?' I asked.

But like I had thought, neither of them moved or said a word. I gathered up the tissues and held a few to my still bleeding hand.

'I'm going now,' I told Corinne.

She staggered over and opened the door for me, carrying a half-empty bottle of vodka. 'Did you hurt yourself?' she cried out, as if she was noticing it for the first time. 'That's terrible, is it bad?' I almost wished she'd fall down, she's unsteady as it is, but she doesn't.

She followed me out on to the street, drinking from her bottle. 'Are you not talking to me,' she asked, very loudly. 'Are you pissed off with me, or something?'

I didn't know whether to be pleased that she came with me instead of staying with him or angry with her for the way she was going on. There were people around and they were looking at her. And now, on top of everything else, I had to get her home in one piece. Yes, concentrate on that. No point in thinking about the other stuff right now.

'Corinne, give me that bottle. You've had enough,' I said.

Anyone who heard me would have thought I was the big sister and she was a kid. Head-wrecking idea.

'Fuck off.'

'Give it to me I said. You can't bring that on the bus with you.'

She walked into a lamppost and cursed. I took advantage of her disorientation to slip the bloody bottle out of her hand and I put it inside someone's gate when she wasn't looking. 'You bitch,' she said when she realized what I'd done. I didn't answer her. My hand had almost stopped bleeding, but it looked a mess, and now I had to drag her down to the bus stop.

'What's wrong with you?' she asked.

'What do you think?'

'Oh, your hand. Well that's what you get for coming over. Why did you come, anyway?'

'I was under the impression that you hated Rob, and I wanted to find out why,' I told her dryly.

I didn't even feel guilty anymore about the things I hadn't told her, especially that Rob had let slip he knew what had happened in the pub. We were getting dirty looks from people. Not surprising, we must have looked a right sight, me with the blood-stained hand carrying her. And it wasn't even the early hours of the morning.

'You can't help me,' she said. 'Like I keep telling you, I just feel the way I do because I do, and your going to see Rob isn't going to change that.'

'But you told me you hated Rob,' I said.

'I did hate him.'

'And then I find you in his flat.'

'Yes, you did find me there. I don't know why. I just felt the need to see him,' she answered.

The way she said it pissed me off. It was like I was a baby that couldn't understand and didn't have to have the discrepancy explained to me.

'You just felt the need to see him! Like he just felt the need to follow Shane home on the bus. Do you think I came down in the last shower or what?' I asked her.

She tripped and fell, almost pulling me down with her. Then she clenched my arm as I pulled her up: 'If you don't want to believe me, then you should stop thinking about all this. But whatever you do, don't let it drive you away, because I don't know what I'd do then. You see, you're the only one I can talk to.'

Corinne was emotional, as if she meant every word of it. From the time I was eleven, she often used to tell me that I was the only one she could talk to. Even if she didn't talk to me all that much after the night of that party. But hearing her say that again did make me less angry with her, even though I felt my anxiety about her intensify to explosion point.

'What about Rob?' I asked, thinking how close they had looked in the flat. Surely she could talk to him.

'I don't know him. Or Shane. Or anyone,' she said.

She meant that too. What was I to do with her? The force of my anxiety was on the verge of smashing this shimmering, icy street.

'Corinne, why do you think you couldn't remember the party right last night?' I asked, reckoning there was a connection between this and her 'not knowing' the two lads.

'What are you talking about?' she asked, upset and genuinely confused.

'Do you not remember? We were talking about that party you brought me to when I was twelve.'

'Yeah I know, it made me sick,' she said, interrupting me.

'But you, you got it wrong. You said he'd put piles of heavy jewellery on me and was on top of me in that chair.'

'No I didn't,' she said, sounding totally shocked.

I was completely frozen. In my ears, I could still hear what she said last night.

'Oh you did,' I said.

'I'm telling you, I didn't. I remember you saying something about the party alright, but I didn't say one word about it. In fact, all you said was "Shane's house reminds me of the party" and then I ran off to the bathroom. I definitely did not say anything about it, never mind go describing it anything like what you said.'

'Corinne, you're lying!' I said, wanting to fling the burning weight of her off my arm but not feeling capable of it.

'Will you fuck off and leave me alone. I am not lying. Can't you see how locked I am, do you really think I'd be able to lie in a state like this?' she asked angrily.

'And do you think I just imagined you saying all that then?' I answered.

I stared at the cars going up and down the road – I'm not imagining them, am I? I absorbed the scene before me, closed my eyes on it and then re-opened them, just to prove to myself that I wasn't imagining the cars or the road, that they were really there.

'Well you must be imagining it,' said Corinne. 'You know, I think you're obsessed by me because it gives you an excuse not to think about your own problems. What have you done about yourself since the night I tried to kill myself? You went to college, but so what? It's not as if you're ever in there, is it?'

It was like we were two birds locked into a cage together and pecking each other's eyes out. Only I didn't see what I had done to set her off. What could I have said to make her turn on me?

'You see what I mean?' continued Corinne. 'You haven't done anything about your music. And for all I know, you're still cutting yourself. Are you?'

No, don't argue with her here and now, you have to get her on this bus. It's pretty empty, thank God. But I'm completely cold now, I can't think of anything to say.

Something struck me: 'What about Danielle? You made it look like there was something going on between you and Rob.'

'Who's Danielle?'

'Rob's girlfriend, the one who came in there with me.' I said.

'Oh her. It doesn't matter, they'd have broken up sooner or later. It doesn't matter who was responsible.'

That might well be true, but it was very hard on Danielle. No point in asking Corinne why she said that, though. No point in anything. Corinne was half-unconscious by the time the bus got to our stop. Or acting it. I got her home and rang the doorbell.

'Take her, Mam. I can't have anything more to do with her today,' I said.

Mam looked at Corinne and then at my hand. Without saying anything, she brought Corinne up to bed while I washed my hand and found plasters for it in the bathroom. Then we both went down to the kitchen, where Corinne wouldn't be able to hear us talking.

'What in the name of God did the two of you get up to?' Mam asked.

'Let's just say I went to see a friend and Corinne was there before me, making a fool of us both.'

'What was she doing? Was she drinking?'

'You could say that, yeah.' I answered.

I looked at her, hoping she wouldn't make me go into too much detail. She could tell I didn't want to talk to her, so she thought the worst.

'She wasn't, she wasn't suicidal, was she?' Mam asked.

'No,' I said. I'm upset and uncomfortable. Why did Corinne have to put me in this position? There's no way I can tell Mam everything that's been happening. And besides, it wouldn't make any sense to her.

'How did you hurt yourself, then?' Mam wanted to know.

'I fell carrying her home,' I answered.

'Oh.' She knew she had to accept what I was saying – it would be too difficult for her to think I was lying. 'So you turned up at your friend's and Corinne was there, embarrassing you. And after all that, you had to bring her home. I can understand that you'd be angry, after all that.'

She makes me sound like a bitch, as if I'm not making allowances for my fucked-up sister after all she's done for me over the years. But I'm still not going to tell her anything. Mam'd be far more upset if she knew what had been going on.

'Well, it was just difficult, you know?' I said, trying to suppress some anger. 'It's difficult to know what to do with Corinne.'

'I know,' said Mam, getting worried. 'I never know what to say to her. And to think I was glad to see her heading off out today – she spends way too much time hanging around the house. So do you, for that matter. In fact, I was thinking of bringing Corinne out for a spin somewhere tomorrow. It'd do her good. Do you want to come too?'

'No, but I'd say Corinne'd like to get out alright.'

It was a good idea. After what happened today, it'd be good to put some space between me and Corinne for a while. Oh God. It's always so tense in here, no matter what. It was time to go to the press, get out Mam's vodka and drink it straight.

'Merle, your hands are shaking,' Mam sounded horrified.

I looked down at my hands. Jesus they are shaking, and so, so badly, like a serious, serious state of withdrawal or something. Does that mean I'm going to drop the bottle? Does that mean more blood?

'Oh don't cry love, don't. Must be pretty bad if *you're* crying,' said Mam, getting upset.

'No it's, it's OK. I could do with a drink though,' I said, pouring a large glass and knocking it back.

'Well, don't drink it like that, you'll make yourself sick. Here, mix some Coke with it and bring the lot up to your room, if you want to be on your own.'

She knows there's nothing she can do, and we're both wishing to bloody hell that things were different. Oh God.

'Mam?'

'Yeah?'

'There's no need for you to cry you know.'

She doesn't know what to say to me and I don't know what to say to her. This is what we've come to. There's nothing I can think of doing, though. I turned away and opened the door.

'Merle?'

I turned back.

'You've been very good with her, you know. And it must have been a terrible strain for you, what with everything and all.' There was a terrible silence. 'I'll take her out tomorrow, a nice spin'd do her good alright.'

What do I say? 'That'd be good, Mam,' I said.

But then I went, leaving her alone with her sorrow and confusion, taking my own pain upstairs with the vodka and Coke.

Fourteen

They were gone the following afternoon when I got up. I went into Corinne's room. She had left the windows open and there was a cold wind blowing in, shaking the curtains and the whole place up. Over on the windowsill was her hairbrush, and the wind was making the hairs on it blow up and down with a fierce energy, as if they were alive. Our hair was the same, and so were our brushes. You wouldn't have known whether it was hers or mine. That disturbed me for a minute, because I was kind of reacting against her after all that had happened yesterday. I picked up the brush and was going to throw it across the room, but instead, I put it outside on the windowsill and closed the window, hoping that the wind would blow the brush away. But it didn't. The hairs just kind of tore themselves away from the brush more and rubbed against the window, like they were moths trying to get in to the night-time light. So I touched them through the glass, knowing that if I was the light and they were moths, my touch would burn them the moment I let them in. Then I sank to the floor and thought of blood.

No, I haven't cut myself since Corinne. And I had noticed before yesterday that, by focusing on her, I could push all thoughts of cutting myself aside. But I don't think that was such a bad thing. It's not as if I was using her and her problems as an excuse to distract me from myself, like she said. But why did she say that? There was something desperate about it, as if she was trying to push me away from her, away from something she didn't want me to know. She thinks it's none of my business. Well in the normal course of events it wouldn't be, but Corinne's so disturbed that I just have to make it my business.

Mam and Corinne came back late that afternoon. Corinne went straight into the sitting room and put on the television without saying anything.

'How's your hand today?' Mam asked. 'Corinne was up at the crack of dawn, wandering around the house like a zombie, opening all the windows. And her in a little nightie in this cold weather.' She seemed sad, but in an accepting way, as if this was the natural state of affairs.

Corinne, I said to myself, I have to talk to Corinne. Yesterday may have dislocated me, but she can't push me away. I'm still with her in that grotesque place of hers, and if I talk to her, maybe we could get beyond all this. She might explain everything that's been happening, and then I won't feel displaced anymore. We could integrate everything into some kind of answer that would lift us away from it all.

But you build up what you expect from Corinne and then you don't get it. She was on her own in front of the television, but she was half-asleep and almost half-drunk. She didn't want to talk. Her words were slow, her pronunciation slurred, and her whole speech pattern was distorted and heavy.

So I left her there and went out. Wandered around in the falling darkness. I didn't even realize it was raining until I saw the rain shine against the car headlights.

Mam was gone out when I got back. Corinne was upstairs and she called me to come up to her. She was lying on Mam's bed with the phone in her hand.

'She's just come into the room,' Corinne said into the phone.

'You can talk to her now.' She put the phone down on to a pillow and said to me, 'Who do you think's on the phone?'

I watched Corinne. Her voice was strange, as heavy and dulled as before, but stranger.

'Rob?' I asked. She laughed. 'Shane?' I asked. She laughed again.

She picked up the phone and held it to her mouth. 'She doesn't know who you are,' she said. 'She's been talking about you for the last few days, and she still hasn't guessed who you are.'

Outside, the rain got heavier. Corinne had left Mam's window wide open and the rain was pouring into the room. I had a heightened sense of that rain, as if it was made up of hundreds of tiny arrows that hit everything except Corinne and the phone.

'He wants to talk to you about the party,' she told me. 'He even remembers you after all this time, and that's quite a compliment, coming from someone like him.'

I stood over at the window, feeling the arrows of rain, but also the cold air that distinguishes the world outside from this room inside. Corinne buried the phone in the pillow when she saw that I'd no intention of taking the phone and said: 'Come on. I don't feel sick anymore after talking to him, and you won't either, trust me.'

I grabbed the phone, meaning to hang it up, but he had beaten me to it: the line was buzzing.

'You shouldn't have taken so long coming to the phone,' said Corinne.

I felt like cutting the line and throwing the phone out the window. But I didn't.

'Jesus Christ, Corinne! You're off your fucking head!' I shouted.

The room seemed to be swirling round and round. I sat on the floor to steady myself. To try and reconcile the image I used to

128

have of my sister with the image of this thing on the bed. Could the girl who said I was the only one she could talk to and who used to let me wear all her clothes have come to this? Maybe she had never been the person I thought she was at all.

'I mean, what the hell do you think you're playing at?' I stormed at her.

She didn't answer me, just stared up at the ceiling.

'Come on, Corinne. You're not getting away with this,' I continued.

Again she didn't answer. Exasperated, I decided to calm down and approach her through her own logic.

'How come you don't feel sick anymore?' I asked her.

'Because I've spoken to him, and that made all the difference. You see, the images of the party meant too much to you. That's why you kept going on about the exact details, saying that I'd painted the wrong picture of it when I hadn't said anything. So I decided you had to talk to him, because hearing him at this stage in your life would have painted a new picture of him and then you would have known that what happened at the party is only an old image in your head. And old images can be controlled and pushed away, so that you don't care about them anymore.'

Corinne had talked about wanting to manipulate images before – on Sunday, when she ran up that lane after seeing that drunk. This hang-up about images is her problem, not mine. But I do often think in images. And I've a very clear, visual memory of what happened at that party. So, in Corinne's state of mind, it would be reasonable enough for her to think it was the details of what happened that mattered to me most. After all, I attacked her the other night because she didn't describe what had happened right – she gave me the wrong image of that night. So what, though. Yesterday, when I told her that she'd given me the wrong description, she denied it completely. She didn't even remember what she'd said.

'You're the one that has a problem with images,' I told her. 'On Sunday afternoon, you ran up that lane all freaked out, saying that you wanted to change the images in your head. What bad memories are giving *you* terrible images?'

'I try to keep my images away from you,' she said. 'Whereas you had to go and fuse your bad images with the stuff I told you. Why did you have to fuse your image of the party with Shane's house and with Rob?'

'You never told me anything. And I never even mentioned Rob in relation to that party!'

'Of course you did,' she said.

'No, I never said anything about him.'

'You did yesterday, when you were telling me that I'd remembered the party wrong, even though I hadn't said a word about it,' Corinne said, sounding so sure of herself.

'I'm telling you. I didn't once mention his name in relation to that party,' I reiterated. Corinne was looking confused now. 'But why do you think I did?' I asked her. 'Is there something between you and him and Shane that reminds you of the party?'

That made her angry: 'You see what I mean! You keep digging in on me, thinking I'm hiding something when there's nothing there. You're just doing this to keep your mind off your own problems. Do you think I wanted to ring your man? No. I felt sick just thinking about it, but I needed to do something dramatic so that I could shake up you and your memories and make you leave me alone!'

Leave her alone, when she said yesterday that I was the only one she could talk to. She's psycho, contradicting herself all over the place and never noticing it. I picked up the phone and shoved it under the bed where I couldn't see it. But I could still see her. I could still see her turning the responsibility for that disgusting phone call back on to me, as if it was my fault. And I could hear her warning me to leave her alone. I left the room.

Living with Corinne could make you paranoid, stop you knowing who you are or what's really happening. All this, and she's only home a week. I reckon it's just about proof that there is something dark between her, Rob and Shane alright. But the question is, even if it is possible to find out what that is, can I bear to do it?

I felt a serious depression falling on me, a need to break away from Corinne, away from that bond that had always been there. No matter how much the two incidents with her friends had pulled us apart, the bond had always remained. But now, I needed to be separate from her. I was almost afraid of pushing Corinne any further, afraid of what she'd do next. And I was ashamed of that, especially when I reminded myself that she had wanted to die and that she could well want to die again without my being able to do anything about it.

Fifteen

The sun shone cold and sharp as nails the following day. I stayed upstairs in bed, because I didn't want to see Corinne and I couldn't motivate myself to go out or go to college. Eventually though, it all got too heavy. So I got up and hovered between the window and the bed, smoking and feeling imprisoned by the closed bedroom door that was keeping Corinne out. I got restless to the point of an anxiety that insisted on being released by doing something but couldn't settle on what to do, so I flitted between the guitar and the CD player without being able to spend more than a few distracted seconds on each. Sometime in the early afternoon, Corinne went out with Mam, so I was able to go downstairs for food, but I didn't feel any less constrained and was relieved when the doorbell rang around an hour later. It was Hannah, just back from college. Today was Monday, and I hadn't seen her since this day last week, when we went to see Shane. The guilt hit me as I realized how bad that looked – Hannah had no idea what had been going on here in the last few days, so she must have thought I was ignoring her. I didn't know what to say to her, but she spoke first.

'You haven't gone to college in ages,' she said, sounding concerned, but almost as if she'd rather not know what had been happening.

'No. And I should have gone over to see how you were, but I couldn't,' I told her.

'Couldn't?' I was worrying her. 'How's Corinne?' she asked, taking it for granted that Corinne must be in a bad way.

'You don't want to know,' I said, grabbing my jacket and closing the door behind me.

'That bad?' said Hannah. 'What's wrong with her?'

'I don't know,' I said, moodily fiddling with my past-it lighter and its weak, raindrop size flame before lighting up a smoke.

She silently took the lighter from me, and waited until she had lit up herself before asking quietly, 'It doesn't have anything to do with Shane, does it?'

'I don't know. In fact, Corinne says there's no reason for the way she is, and I don't know what to make of her. I mean, she can't have been born like that. Seeing Shane on Monday doesn't seem to have directly caused anything she's done this week, if that's what you're wondering, but I don't know.'

And I wasn't really sure I wanted to know either, not after yesterday. As we walked under the hardness of the blue sky, I managed to scrape out a full account of the last few days from inside of me. An account including that party and the other bad night I'd spent with Corinne's friends – stuff that had never seen the light of Hannah's day before.

'How come you never told me about that before,' she asked.

'But it wasn't a question. She understood why I hadn't told her. She understood that I hadn't been able to, and that I was only telling her now so that she'd have some idea what Corinne was like. No matter how unwilling Hannah might be to help, she knew I was appealing to her to do whatever she could think of that would help with Corinne.

'Corinne's more disturbed than I thought,' she said. 'And I definitely think there's something awful between her and Rob. I always reckoned there was something weird about him, but I could never put my finger on it, because it was just a feeling. But whatever it is, I don't think it has anything to do with Shane, because, because . . .' Hannah drifted into silence in an attempt to formulate what she had to say. I waited anxiously, and eventually what she said was, 'Can you come with me now and we'll go and see Shane?'

'Yeah, why?' I asked.

I was pretty stunned by this. I'd definitely go though. Hannah was obviously offering me what I had appealed to her for, even though it was difficult for her to do so. What is it? There's so much I want to know about Shane, and so much she obviously hasn't told me yet.

Hannah spoke nervously, which wasn't like her at all. 'I felt really bad after I came home on Monday night. I kept thinking and thinking about Shane and about what a disaster our going to see him had been. So I decided that I needed to go back over there, on my own, just to say to him, "Well, here you are. And I don't know you, but, even if I never see you again, I just want to say, I'm your sister and I hope everything works out for you." So I went back there the next day.'

I couldn't believe it. Hannah had said on Monday that she might go back to see him sometime, but from the very reluctant way she'd been acting about him up to then, there was no way I'd have thought she'd have gone back so soon.

'And how did it go?'

She shrugged vaguely, almost emotionlessly you would have thought, unless you had noticed how tense she was, the way she was chain-smoking and clenching my lighter in her left fist. 'He says he doesn't know anything about Corinne or Rob, and that the reason he was so hostile when we met him was because it was such a shock to see us and he didn't know what to do,' she said.

It was impossible to tell from that what exactly had happened, or if Hannah really believed what she had just said, because she was hiding behind a toneless, expressionless voice.

'But on Monday, he showed more of a reaction to Corinne than he did to you,' I said, wondering what kind of an answer she'd give to that.

'I'd say that's because they're the same age. He probably feels a bit more sensitive about her because they were in the same class in school and all,' she muttered, still hiding.

'But you're his sister.' I said.

It's typical of Hannah to mentally twist situations the way she wants them. But surely even she can't deny the fact that, in the normal course of events, someone is going to show more of a reaction to a sister that he hasn't seen for years than to just another classmate. This conversation got cut off here though, because we were in sight of the bus stop and had to run to catch an approaching bus.

'I believed Shane when he told me he hadn't seen either Rob or Corinne in years,' Hannah said on the bus. 'And you will too, once . . . once you've met him properly. But all I'll say now is that you'll be surprised.'

I didn't ask her why. Not when she was like this, it wasn't worth it. Even though I couldn't think what she could possibly mean. But I believed her when she said I'd get a surprise – the new Shane had already been something of a surprise when we saw him on Monday, and I'd say that the explanations behind how he got to be like that could well provide some more surprises. But I wasn't sure that the surprise Hannah was talking about would convince me that Shane had no dark, past connection with Rob and Corinne. All the same, I burned with impatience the whole way over to Shane's. Hannah remained withdrawn, staring blankly at the clouded-up window beside her. She didn't once reach over to clear a view for herself, like I would have.

Eventually, we got to Shane's bus stop. Walked silently once more in the shadow of unusually dark, heavy trees, kicking our way through mounds of dead leaves. Hannah paused anxiously at the gate before flinging it open. It made a loud, grating noise that would have chilled my blood had I not been so wound up. It chilled Hannah though, making her delay a few moments before following me up the steep granite steps to the front door. She knocked twice. For all its bulk, the twisted metal knocker produced only a dull, muffled sound. No one answered. You'd think they'd at least have a bell, I muttered to myself. Hannah took a deep breath and knocked again. This time a man answered – kind of fat, and so tall that he filled the doorway, almost blotting out the dark hall behind him. I reckoned he was in his fifties. He had grey hair and dark clothes that matched the air all around him. He looked from me to Hannah and back again before smiling politely.

'Hello Hannah, it's good to see you,' he said pleasantly. His accent was American.

Hannah smiled nervously. 'Thanks,' she said. 'I'm sorry to bother you again so soon, but we had to talk to you today. This is Merle, and . . .'

'Oh, right,' he said, looking at me as if he'd known who I was all along. 'Come in, come in,' he said, stepping back out of the doorway so that there was room for us to make our way in behind him.

I followed them into a big room. The man pulled back the heavy wine velvet curtains to let the daylight in through large windows facing each other at the front and the back of the room. Even so, the curtains blocked out half the light, and the room was still dark.

'That's better,' he said. 'You must excuse us, but we're not long out of bed. Sit down, please.'

136

Hannah obediently sat on a wine velvet couch and I sat beside her.

'Can I offer you both tea? Coffee?' he asked, standing in the middle of the floor.

'Tea, please,' we said, and he left the room, saying he wouldn't be long.

'Who is he?' I asked Hannah.

'His name's Mr Johnson,' she said.

I'd gotten the feeling he'd be a Mr alright.

'Yeah, but who is he?' I urged. 'Are him and Shane . . .?'

'Yeah,' she said.

'So it was him that was with Shane that night in the pub then?'

'Well, yeah, but the thing is . . .' Hannah began, but just then, the door opened and Mr Johnson came back in with the tea and stuff, putting the tray down on a dark wooden table.

'That was quick,' said Hannah, trying self-consciously to be friendly. She got up and took both our cups, pouring my tea for me and remembering to give me only a tiny drop of milk. Mr Johnson sat facing us, in an elaborate armchair beside the smoky-grey marble fireplace.

'So,' he said. 'You're Merle. And your sister, then, is Corinne.'

'Yes,' I said, staring right at him. Even though he was smiling, I felt uncomfortable. Hannah's obviously told him all about me, whereas I don't know anything about him. How the hell am I meant to ask someone like him about Corinne?

'Such pretty names,' he continued. 'Wherever did your mother find them?'

I shrugged. 'I don't know, she just liked them.' But I felt that was a bit curt, so I added 'I'm called after some actress I've never heard of.'

'Yes, yes,' he said. 'Merle Oberon. She goes back a while, doesn't she? In fact, I'm sure she would have been before your mother's time too . . .' and he broke off there, acting as if it was such an interesting fact that he had to think about it now for a while.

'Merle's the French for blackbird as well,' I said, wanting to fill the silence like I always did when I got nervous.

'I see,' he said, sounding almost too fascinated. 'I didn't know that.'

'Yeah, well, I looked it up in a name dictionary once,' I said.

He continued to smile as he took another drink of his coffee. The subject of my name had been pretty much exhausted, and I wondered was he going to get on to Corinne's next, but instead he said, 'Oh, and my name's Johnson, by the way.'

'Yeah, Hannah told me,' I said.

'Right,' he said. 'Well, it's nice to meet you after hearing so much about you.'

Just what had Hannah told him? I lit up a smoke, hoping that it would help me think more clearly, and then regretted it when I saw there were no ashtrays around. I didn't want to flick ash all over this lumpy, uncomfortable couch or the dark rug that had a twisted and tangled pattern and accusing eyes of its own.

'Sorry,' I said. 'Do you mind if I smoke?'

'Not at all,' he said. 'Go right ahead. We don't smoke here, but you're very welcome to. Let me just see if I can find you something you can use as an ashtray.'

He got up, looked around, and then walked over to the mantelpiece, where he picked up a shiny black marble box covered in blue and white birds.

'Here, use this,' he said, opening it and handing it to me.

'Oh I couldn't,' I said. 'It's too nice.'

'You like it?' he asked. 'Then keep it, it's yours.'

'Oh no,' I said, embarrassed. 'It looks expensive.'

'It's just a little something I picked up downtown last week,' he assured me.

'Take it, Merle,' said Hannah. 'You could use it to put plectrums in. She plays guitar,' she said, turning to Mr Johnson.

'Oh yeah?' he asked me.

I nodded as I emptied my smokes out of their box so that I could use that for my ash instead of my new present. Imagine him just giving me this, I thought.

'I'm afraid music's not really my thing,' he said.

'What are you interested in?' asked Hannah quickly.

'Oh, this and that,' he said. 'Before you dropped by, I was just going to take a look at a book on Paris.'

'Is that where you were on holiday?' Hannah asked. He frowned at her questioningly, so she explained slightly nervously that Shane had mentioned being away the first time she'd spoken to him here.

'Oh,' he said. 'No, we just took a couple of weeks in Cyprus, because your Irish summer had been so bad. But I was thinking of taking a trip to Paris, maybe sometime in the spring.'

'Oh, lovely,' said Hannah. 'I've never been there myself, but I'd love to go sometime.'

'Yes, you should,' he told her. 'Would you like to have a look at my book?'

He took down a large, glossy hardback book from a book case at the back of the other part of the room. Bewildered, I sat there as Hannah opened the book and handed me one side of it so that I could look at the pictures too. What's going on here? I wondered. He doesn't seem to have the slightest interest in why we came, and he hasn't even mentioned Shane once. Where is Shane? Hannah had flicked over to a section on the art galleries and was looking at some of the paintings. I tried to focus on them, hoping that it would clear my head. Some of them were pretty cool. I stared at one of them, which showed a night sky alive with stars. You never saw stars that clearly in real life, though. I wondered what the sky had been like the night

Corinne saw Shane in the pub, and that made me decide to bring up the subject here and now.

'So did you meet my sister then?' I asked Mr Johnson.

'I'm sorry?' he asked, startled.

Uncomfortably, I went on, 'it's just, my sister told me that she met Shane and some older man in a pub, and she was obviously talking about you. And, the thing is, she tried to kill herself the next day, so . . .'

'Yes, yes,' he said, sounding perplexed. 'Hannah told me about this, and I don't understand it at all, because I never met your sister.'

'Well, might Shane have been with anyone else that night?' I asked him.

'No,' he said very definitely. 'If Shane goes out at all, he goes out with me.'

'Oh right,' I said. 'Where's Shane now, then?'

There was a small silence and then he answered, 'Upstairs. Why do you ask?'

That was ridiculous. Why shouldn't I ask?

'Oh, I was just wondering, seeing as he's not down here and you said that you always went out together.'

'I see. Well, no. He hasn't sneaked out to meet up with someone else so that they can wreak havoc and push young women to the verge of suicide.' He laughed for a moment and then stopped. 'I'm sorry, I shouldn't laugh about your sister. That is so insensitive of me.'

'Don't worry about it,' I said.

'No really, I am sorry,' he persisted.

'Corinne's been going from bad to worse lately,' said Hannah. 'Merle just doesn't know what to do about her, and she's convinced it all started that night in the pub.'

'Well,' said Mr Johnson. 'I wish there was something I could do to help, but all I can say is that neither myself nor Shane ever met her in that pub.'

'But there must be something in her story,' I insisted.

'Oh?' he asked coolly.

'Well, at first she said that she didn't even speak to you,' I said, kind of flustered by his attitude. 'But then she got so upset that I couldn't make out what she was saying at all, and I wanted to believe that something had happened because I didn't want to believe that she turned around to kill herself just because she was feeling depressed. So I went to see Rob, and he acted as if something had happened alright, so . . .'

'Yes, yes, Hannah told me the whole story, and I don't like the sound of this Rob person at all. He's obviously told you a pack of lies.'

'It wasn't like that, though,' I said. 'In fact, he was doing his best to keep the whole thing quiet.'

Mr Johnson rolled his eyes upwards. 'I imagine he didn't want to get into too much detail in case it became too obvious that he was making the whole thing up.'

'But people don't just turn around and kill themselves for nothing,' I insisted.

Hannah sighed. 'But we know that Corinne was depressed anyway,' she said.

'Not that depressed,' I answered.

'Look,' said Mr Johnson. 'Hannah's right. From what I've heard about your sister, she really needs to go into therapy, and if I were you, I'd concentrate on that and forget about all this other stuff.'

The cheek of him to be so dismissive of people he doesn't even know, I thought, but I didn't say it. There was something about him, he radiated this heavy aura of domination all around the room. Hannah had been soaked in it, and I felt it pressing in on me, silencing me. He remained sitting there, smiling at us. Oh, I don't know what to think, though he has me almost convinced that nothing happened in the pub – I just can't picture him being involved, somehow. But still, there's something else I have to know.

'Just one more thing,' I said. 'You see, I think Corinne's been pretty messed-up since she was sixteen, which was when Shane left home. And he got pretty violent before he left home, so I think it goes to show that something pretty bad happened to them, because why else would they both have been messed-up at the same time?'

'Oh please,' he said impatiently. 'All this is pure speculation.'

'Well if it's OK with you, I'd like to hear it from Shane,' I said.

He scowled at me. 'Can't you just take my word for it?' he asked angrily.

Hannah looked uneasy. She didn't want to alienate him. But seeing as I'd come this far, I thought I'd go a little further.

'Please,' I said. 'It'd mean a lot to me.'

'OK,' he said, kind of pissed off.

Mr Johnson left to get Shane. I walked around the room, trying to shake the weight of it off me. The floorboards were varnished a dark brown, and the carpet was dark. Even though the place was so big, the darkness and the heaviness of the style sucked in what little light penetrated, making the room look enclosed and oppressive. I watched the blurred, grey reflection of the sparkling chandelier in the antique mirror over the fireplace and shivered. In the coldness of that distorting glass, I saw Mr Johnson enter the room, followed by Shane. He looked surprised to see us there, and stood uneasily in the middle of the room, as if he didn't know what to do.

'Hi, Shane!' said Hannah eagerly.

He muttered hello back to us. Mr Johnson sat in the couch beside the fireplace and indicated for Shane to sit beside him. This he did.

'Now Shane,' said Mr Johnson. 'This girl needs your strict reassurance that you were never involved in anything traumatic that happened to her sister, either recently or in the past, and that your leaving home had absolutely nothing to do with her.'

Shane dragged the tip of his shoe forward and backward along the floorboards until Mr Johnson patted him on the arm and told him that there was no need to get upset. Shane scowled at me then and said nervously, 'Look, like I told Hannah the other day, nothing happened. I'm telling you, I don't know the first thing about Rob and Corinne and what they've been up to, and I thought that would have been obvious to you on Monday.'

Mr Johnson patted him approvingly on the arm again. 'There now, you see?' he said, looking at me.

I could see that was all I was going to get, even though I didn't believe Shane. I had thought that I could admire him for transforming himself, but I couldn't. Not when he owed it all to Mr Johnson. It was sickening to see Shane so completely under his thumb. He was even dressed in black as well.

'That's fair enough,' I told Mr Johnson. 'I must say, I think it's great, all you've done for Shane.'

I almost got the impression that Mr Johnson understood I was being sarcastic, but Hannah thought I was being serious. She jumped up and said, 'Oh, it's fantastic, Merle. And Shane designed this room, picked out the colours and the furniture and everything. Isn't it amazing what he can do?'

'Oh yeah,' I answered, looking around the depressing place and wondering if it was really Shane's doing. I fingered one of the candelabras on the mantelpiece and said, 'It must be very atmospheric in here at night.' What I was really thinking was that this place would be even more creepy then than during the day. 'Did you do all the painting and stuff as well?' I asked Shane.

Hannah answered for him. 'Oh no, they got people in for that.

143

But you should see the back-garden, he did that.' she said. 'If, if that's OK with you, that is,' she said, turning to Mr Johnson.

'Well, there's not much to see, but why not?' he said politely, all charm and smiles now that he was back in control of the conversation.

Mr Johnson led us down the dark backstairs into a hall and yanked at the heavy back door in one abrupt movement that counteracted the reluctance of the hinges to open the door. It was unlocked, despite several large bolts and locks.

'Do you not keep that door locked?' I asked, thinking that it was a bit of a waste, fitting all those locks if you were going to leave the door open.

'Not during the day,' said Shane, 'because we're in and out. But I always lock it before going to bed. Anyway, there's not much crime around here.'

I looked at Shane in surprise, this being the first time he had spoken for himself. It was ironic, him talking about the absence of crime.

'And even in the winter, are you out here?' I asked him.

Mr Johnson laughed smoothly. 'Shane's very fond of fresh air.'

We stepped out into a large, bare garden. It was so bright compared to the darkened house that my eyes took some time to adjust. Nevertheless, I wondered what Shane had done out here besides cutting the grass.

'Shane helped to cut down the trees and plant new grass,' said Mr Johnson.

'Where were the trees?' I asked.

'All along the walls,' answered Shane. 'They had to go though, they made the place too dark.'

'Shane weeded the path as well,' said Hannah enthusiastically.

It was sad, really, to be so disproportionately impressed by such a little thing. But then, maybe she was just trying to be as positive as possible about the whole thing. The path's neat slabs led to a door in the back wall. I asked what was behind that door because it had such a rotting and ominous look about it, and it was locked by two threatening new bolts, unlike the open back door. 'A back lane,' said Mr Johnson, before steering us back into the house and up to the hall.

In the darkness, Mr Johnson told Hannah to 'feel free' to drop by anytime, that he'd always be glad to see her. Just call him first, so that he'd know to expect her, he said. Then he shook each of our hands, and said, 'Goodbye now, have a nice day.' Shane hovered in the background. I waved at him in pity as we left, because I didn't like to think of leaving him behind. And then the door closed behind us.

Sixteen

It gave me an incredible sense of release to be outside that house, but all the same, I felt a wave of tiredness hitting me now that it was all over. The gate grated as harshly as before when we opened it, but this time, the late afternoon light seemed to penetrate the trees and fill the street as I started walking away quickly.

'That went OK in the end, didn't it?' said Hannah, catching up on me. 'I mean, it got a bit dodgy there for a while, but it was alright, wasn't it?'

Alright? I rummaged around in my jacket. Only one of my smokes had been broken from being left loose in my pocket. I threw it away, back down the road towards that house, and emptied the ash from the cigarette box so that I could put the other smokes back into it. Then I pulled out the little black box Mr Johnson had given me so that I could have another look at it. I wondered if it was right for me to have taken it.

'It was nice of him to give you that, wasn't it?' said Hannah, looking at the box.

'It was nice of him,' I said, handing it to her.

'So you liked him then?' she persisted. She obviously did anyway.

'Like's a very strong word, Hannah,' I said. But I didn't want to annoy her, so I added, 'All I'll say is that he was very nice, until he got angry with me there when I was asking him about Corinne.'

'You're not pissed off about that, are you?' she asked. 'I mean, it's probably just that he didn't want you upsetting Shane.'

'Why do you like him so much?' I returned, taken by her defensive tone.

'Because of all he's done for Shane, of course. Why do you think?'

'Oh come on, Hannah. I know he's rich and that, but do you really think it's worth it, the way he dominates Shane? Did you notice the way he didn't come down to see us until he was called? And then, when he did come down, he only spoke when he was told to.'

'Oh, that's neither here nor there,' Hannah answered. 'Shane probably didn't know we'd dropped by until he was told, and anyway, I'd say he was mortified at being asked all that stuff in front of Mr Johnson.'

'You see what I mean? You're even calling him Mr Johnson!'

'Well, it's his name,' she said defensively.

It looked like he had Hannah exactly where he wanted her too.

'What did you tell him about me and Corinne?' I asked, remembering the way he kept saying, 'Yes, Hannah told me all about it.'

'I hope you don't mind, Merle,' said Hannah nervously. 'But I had to tell him everything. You see, as soon as I saw him, I knew that it must have been him that Corinne saw with Shane, so I asked him about that night, though I wasn't surprised when he told me that he'd never even met her. But just in case he did know something, I ended up having to tell him everything anyway.'

I could imagine that alright. Him dominating and manipulating the conversation in order to get everything he wanted out of

Hannah and her being too intimidated to say anything other than answer his questions. Jesus Christ, I hate to think that he knows all about me whereas I don't know the first thing about him. Pity I don't know anyone who could tell me. I'd love to know where he got his money, seeing as he doesn't seem to have a job. And more importantly, I'm dying to know where and how he got Shane. But I can see that these questions also loom large in Hannah's mind, and there's no point worrying her any further by discussing them. Silently, I offered her a smoke. She took one and we continued on down the road.

'Do you believe him then, about nothing happening that night?' Hannah asked anxiously.

'Oh, I don't know what to think anymore,' I said. 'I mean, I can't help but think there's something they're not telling me, but if they're all so into keeping it quiet, then there's not much I can do, is there?'

'Not a lot,' Hannah agreed. 'And besides, you have to give up on it some time. Oh, I reckon that something did happen with Rob and Corinne alright, but that seems to be some dark secret between them, and from what you were telling me, it's not a good idea to go pushing them any further about it.'

She was right. The image of last night's phone call collided unpleasantly with that of Mr Johnson and Shane on their couch, denying all knowledge of Corinne. I don't think I can take this tension anymore. I can't take the pressure of being with Corinne and doing all this – building everything up in the hope that it'll explode and reveal everything to me and then it not happening.

'So was Mr Johnson the surprise you were talking about?' I asked Hannah.

'He was, yeah,' she said. 'I reckoned that once you'd met him and seen what he'd done for Shane, you'd know that neither of them were the sort of people who'd be involved in whatever you think must have happened to screw Corinne up so badly.'

I'm not so sure about that. Mr Johnson was a bit too anxious to keep Corinne out of the conversation. Hannah thinks this was because he didn't want to upset Shane, probably because the fabric of his new life was so recently and so delicately woven that it could easily be torn. And maybe she's right. But still. Maybe it's just that I don't want to take the obvious explanation, but I remember how hostile Shane was to Corinne on Monday, and I definitely think there's something in it.

'Oh, you wouldn't know,' I said to Hannah. 'Having said that, I don't have a clue what could have happened. All I know is that it must be bad.'

'Mmm,' she said. 'You don't think there's anything in what Corinne said about being freaked out at the sight of Shane with Mr Johnson. Especially if she thought Shane was doing business . . .'

'No,' I said. 'Because I don't believe she just saw them. And she tried to tell me something when I said it to her, only I couldn't make out what she was saying.'

'Yeah, but still,' said Hannah. 'It would have been a bit of a shock to see something like that. I mean, it's even a bit of a shock to see it the way it is. Because you have this set vision of Shane the druggie and then, you see him six years later, and he's looking really well, but he's with this bloke. And well, it kind of throws you a bit, doesn't it?'

'Oh it's unnerving alright, to think of Shane as your man's live-in lover. But that's no reason to kill yourself. Or to stalk the house, for that matter, like Rob did.'

'But what do you want to do then?' she asked, genuinely concerned. 'I mean, what can you do? You've tried everything already.'

We turned the corner and went to walk down towards the bus stop. I was relieved to be getting out of the area, but I didn't want to go home, I didn't know what to do there. Where'll I go though? I'm too tired to go anywhere, and besides, I don't want to go off on Hannah after her going to all the trouble of bringing me here.

'I know you think this has got nothing to do with it,' said Hannah. 'But Corinne said herself that she wanted to die because she couldn't feel anything for her boyfriend, and I've always thought there was something in that, because Corinne never used to go out with anyone properly. Why don't you ask her about that?'

Because I didn't think that was the problem. And in any case, I didn't feel up to it – God only knows what Corinne'll do if I start asking her more personal questions.

'She told me that the relationship was an example of her problems, not the cause of them,' I said. 'It was like, she was feeling this complete detachment and lack of emotional connection to everything around her, including her boyfriend, and she just stressed that particular example when she was talking to me because relationships are the sort of thing people expect you to react strongly to.'

Oh she has a way with her words alright, so good that you can't see them for what they really are underneath. You just see them as a glinting edge on the walls she has up against you and all you can do is accept them as that because she won't let you come any closer to her.

Hannah thought about it. 'So what do you think then?' she asked doubtfully.

'Oh, I don't know Hannah. I don't know anything anymore.'

I didn't seem to be able to challenge anything anymore. For the first time, I didn't think that, sooner or later, I could make a difference to Corinne. I just didn't know what to do. And I could tell that Hannah was seriously worried about me, the way she was looking at me.

'Come on,' she said, pulling a phone number out of her pocket and walking in the direction of a phone box. 'It's about time you did something to take your mind off all that. I wasn't going to say this to you until I found out what the story was with you and Corinne and that, but, when I was walking around here on Tuesday, I saw this ad in a shop from a cover band looking for a guitarist. This band play in a pub in town on a Tuesday night, and I thought it might be a nice thing for you to do. Just until something better comes along.'

'Hannah, I don't want to be in a cover band,' I said. But I appreciated the thought.

She dialled the number. 'Oh come on, you could do with a laugh.'

She was right there. So I let Hannah go ahead, even though I didn't really care much for the idea. I listened to her talking on the phone, getting directions to some place. Then she excitedly told me that the band hadn't found a guitarist yet.

As chance would have it, they were only a ten-minute walk away. The band was two girls and a fella in a back shed behind a two-storey house. The girl who played the drums told us that the old guitarist, who was her cousin, was leaving the band because he'd gotten a new job in Galway. In fact, he was leaving so soon that he wouldn't be able to play the gig on Tuesday, so they were stuck. Would I be ready that soon, they asked me anxiously. Oh yeah, I told them. I knew the songs – Beatles and the like – from way back, and they were dead easy anyway. So after an hour or two jamming, me and Hannah headed off home.

When I got home, I ignored Corinne in the kitchen, and went straight upstairs, turning the key in my bedroom door. I don't like being locked this close to you Corinne. It doesn't leave much room for anything else, especially when the whole thing is so dark. I have to stay out of your world, at least for a while. I can't accept you without questioning you, so it's just too dangerous for me.

Different worlds. After that party when I was twelve, me and Corinne slipped into a new phase: I stayed out of her world and she told me nothing about it. When at thirteen, I finally got a guitar, I kept Corinne out of that too.

I remember my first guitar lesson with my uncle's friend. I had met him once or twice before at Christmas piss-ups in our gaff. He was in his forties, and played country and western in a local pub on a Sunday night. Corinne laughed herself stupid at the thought of my going to him, saying she'd disown me on the spot if she had to listen to me playing that stuff. I ignored her, telling her he'd be a hell of a lot better as a teacher than any of her friends would be. Anyway, my uncle had told me that his friend knew everything about all kinds of music. He taught guitar and keyboard to loads of kids around where I lived, and they all thought he was great. He was completely off his head, but always in good form. He might forget what day of the week it was, and that you were meant to be coming for a lesson, but you'd hardly ever miss out on getting your class because he'd usually be around the house anyway.

He asked me what kind of stuff I wanted to play, and I said rock stuff, I suppose. He thought that was kind of funny, the way I said it, and said fair enough, once we got set up, and I knew some chords and stuff, we'd start off with the Beatles, because that's what he did with everyone else. Then I remember that he looked at me, and asked was that what I really wanted to do? I said that, when you listen to songs, sometimes the guitar is just backing up the words, and it's not important. I like it when the guitar's important, when it's doing something in its own right. I like proper playing. OK he said, you want to learn lead, and you want to learn blues – that's the best way to learn guitar, because the blues are where it all comes from.

And it may have taken some time and a lot of sore fingers, but I eventually got to be good.

Hannah and the girls thought I was so cool. Corinne didn't comment on my playing, but she did tell me to get into a band. And I told her that I would in my own time, that I was still only learning. I didn't like her to hear me practising. She made me nervous. Even then, I could sense a lethal edge in her that pushed me away, although I still felt locked into a bond with her. I didn't mind anyone else listening to me. Even so, I did my best stuff on my own, or when I knew that Corinne was out.

I'm remembering those nights, now that I want to turn in on myself and switch everything else off. It's not easy to keep everything out, though. There's too much going on. I'm haunted by images of Shane imprisoned in that awful house. And images of Corinne and Rob, bound somehow together in that flat of his with the broken mirror. It's not easy at all. None of that lifted from me until night, when I was working in Spar, tired and bored out of my mind. I switched off while I was watching the sliding glass doors in the rain. When the doors were closed, I watched the rain blur the street outside. When the doors opened, the rain poured in and I felt the cold of the outside. And it had a strangely calming effect.

Maybe it's only wishful thinking, believing that there's a connection between Corinne, Rob, and Shane and the way they are. Maybe they're just like that naturally and I'm looking for excuses to justify it all because I want things to be different. Hannah's right. I'll only make things worse if I push Corinne and them any further. So I might as well just concentrate on something else. Thinking about the cover band and the gig on Tuesday is constructive, it should be able to pull my mind away from all that, but I can't feel it happening. Oh it'll happen alright.

Hannah says, what about the boyfriend? Nothing struck me about him from anything Corinne said, but I remember she had another boyfriend, when she was fifteen. And she was weird about him too, I remember that.

I feel as if walking away from all this is some kind of a betrayal. It's crazy really, because I don't owe Corinne anything. She owes me, more like. And the way she sees it, I'd be doing her a favour if I left off. Why does it feel so wrong then? It shouldn't – I spent several years keeping my life separate from hers, so I should be able to do it again. Maybe it's because I thought we had bridged that division, before she tried to kill herself. But we couldn't have, really. She wasn't even living in Dublin, and more importantly, it never even occurred to her to tell me how messed-up she was before she did it, even though I told her about my problems. It's probably not fair of me to have expected her to tell me if she was in a bad way, but still. I know I'm a fine one to talk, seeing as I reacted so coldly to the thought of her death, but I've gone beyond that now – these last few weeks of relentless searching for reasons and explanations have long since thrown off those icy shadows.

Leave her be and walk away. Hannah's right, this band should be good for a laugh. I can do different worlds again. It used to be that the only world I gave recognition to was one that was completely separate from Corinne's. It consisted of me and Hannah when we were younger. We used to go out a lot, hang around the shops and different estates. We got to know a lot of people. Hannah told everyone how good I was on the guitar, and they used to come up to the gaff to hear me. They all asked why wasn't I in a band, and I said I was waiting till I found the right one.

I was still fourteen when I got to hear about Aidan, the singer everyone fancied. That was the Aidan I ended up going out with for three years, and I never once discussed him with Corinne until that night at the end of this summer, when I told her about the break-up and how I used to cut myself to calm myself down.

That was the night when she should have told me about her problems.

Anyway, when me and Hannah met Aidan for the first time, we could see why all the girls were mad about him. We didn't really get talking to him that day, because he had so many people around him, but we were told that the band would be playing at this thing in the Community Centre that Sunday afternoon, and me and Hannah said that we would definitely go.

It was summer at the time, when you got the chance to mess around more than usual and to sit around thinking about things. And me and Hannah spent a lot of time discussing exactly what I was going to do. It was great crack. We used to sit in my room for hours with the door locked and the cigarettes lit and the music down low in case anyone wanted us.

'Peter and Dara from school are always asking you to be in a band with them. You could do that, I suppose,' said Hannah.

'Neither of them can play though – Peter's always talking about learning the guitar, but he still hasn't gotten around to it,' I said.

'What happened with that girl Tracy who learned to play on her brother's drums?' Hannah asked.

'I met her and we jammed. I told you about that, didn't I? Then she said that she'd see about us getting together with some people she knew, but I haven't heard back from her since.'

I was looking forward to Aidan's gig all night Saturday when we were out drinking. Summer drinking was the best, because it wasn't cold, and everyone was always more laid-back. Me and Hannah were talking to this girl, Áine, who knew Aidan and them very well. She said that they had a good band going, and that he was an amazing singer. What she was saying made me look forward to the next day even more.

Hannah stayed over with me that night, and we had some vodka left over, so we locked the bedroom door and ended up staying up half the night. That meant that we slept in the following day. I woke up some time after two and panicked because the gig was at three and it was a good twenty-minute walk down to the Community Centre.

'Hannah, wake up, we're going to be dead late,' I told her.

By the time I got her fully awake, she was still sluggish and cranky and didn't want to go anywhere, 'Because we'll be rushing and I won't have time to wash my hair.'

'You don't need to wash your hair, you washed it yesterday,' I said.

'But it always feels dirty after going out.'

'Ah Hannah, you know how much I want to go.'

She got up, making faces. 'I'm coming, I'm coming. Did I say I wasn't?'

We were twenty minutes late, but the band hadn't been on yet. Hannah slumped on to a chair at the back, saying, 'For fuck sake, all that rushing for nothing.'

'Well, at least we haven't missed them,' I said.

We were both wrecked, and it wasn't exactly comfortable, sitting on those little upright chairs. The hall was dusty and stuffy, with bright sun pouring in the windows and making it worse. It was the kind of warmth that made you feel filthy and sweaty after a night out, especially when you were half-asleep. There was another band on who didn't have a clue. The guitars were out of tune and there was a terrible grating feedback from the amps that killed our ears. After the song started, they had to stop for the guitarist to remember the chords, and then when they started up again, everyone was out of time with everyone else. It was brutal, and I was wondering how much of this we were going to have to sit through.

But just as me and Hannah were debating going into the toilets and staying there until we heard some more promising noises, that band finished up, and Aidan came on. And they were really good. So good that I'd have given my eye teeth to be in that band with him. But when we met them after the gig, I saw that they were all really good friends, so I reckoned there was no way either of the two guitarists would ever leave, and I tried to forget about ever being in that band with Aidan. But I got lucky. Because a few months later, I heard that the lead guitarist was moving down the bog, so he'd have to leave the band. And one day, I got talking to Aidan about letting me join. And that was it: I was in.

The first two years in the band were great. Me and Hannah had such a good time, hanging around with the band, arranging gigs in obscure pubs in town and making everyone we knew go to them so that we could pay the hiring costs. And it seemed a matter of course that I should end up going out with Aidan. Everyone else expected it. I didn't see him like the other girls did. I thought he was extremely good-looking, of course, but it was a bit like what Corinne had said about her recent boyfriend: I knew he was attractive and that I should feel attracted to him, but I didn't. I worried about it a lot, but eventually I decided that I must fancy him, even if I was unemotional about it, because I was so dependent on him – I needed to be going out with him, I didn't like it any other way. We had a few little break-ups over the years because he was with other girls, and I was miserable until we were back together again.

It was only coming up to the big, and final, break-up that I accepted we shouldn't be going out with each other. Things changed so much. Aidan got so difficult to be with, and he was lazy about everything – it wasn't just the band he messed up on, he practically failed the Leaving because he didn't do a tap of work. The last year was so bad that it was no wonder I ended up a psychological wreck with my razor blades. If I ever fancied anyone, it was Rob. And to be honest, I was glad at the time that

I didn't stand a chance with him. I had my own balances built up between life and possibility and I didn't want them disturbed.

But that was all over now. Corinne was over. And Hannah was still there like she'd always been. It had looked for a while as if I had alienated her, because of the way I had insisted on looking for Shane, but I reckon she was glad now that I had done that. She was much happier about him than she'd ever been, and for some reason, she'd taken to Mr Johnson in a big way. She was still there for me. We'd always meant so much to each other, because together we had had a life away from the complications of her brother and my sister. Though she hadn't known then about the things that had happened to me with Corinne's friends. I was so glad I had finally told her – I think it made her understand things better, and it pushed her into bringing me over to Shane's.

Now's the time to walk away again. I'll do the cover band for a while, give myself a different focus.

But no matter how hard I tried to push them aside, Corinne, Rob, and Shane remained, colouring and clouding my vision.

Seventeen

Stars shone with unusual clarity that Tuesday night. I packed up all my stuff for the gig and brought it downstairs, hesitating outside the sitting room door where Corinne was, watching television. No, I won't say goodbye to her – she's been avoiding me just as much as I've been avoiding her. Such a pity that it has come to this. I rubbed my eyes – the sleepless nights and the emotional strain of living in the same house with all that had been done and all that was being left unsaid were exhausting. I went across the road and called for Hannah. She answered the door, all done up in her good black dress.

'You look great,' I told her, thinking how I was just in my normal clothes. 'I should have made more of an effort myself, only I didn't think of it.'

'Oh you look grand,' she said. 'The only reason I got all dressed up is because I haven't been out in ages – not properly anyway.'

No, not since before Corinne tried to kill herself, and that felt like years ago. Time to try and push it all away, if only for a night. Me and Hannah left in the smooth air that seemed to shine like melting ice in a glass. We were both in good form, and the street lamps lit our path with the lustre of promise.

The night spilled into the dingy pub in town, dressing it up in a glossy, dry ice mist. The small stage, the rest of the band and the small, chatting audience all faded into the mist while I played.

And for a time, a trance-like peace co-existed strangely with my vibrant, almost violent, chords and notes.

Hannah sat alone on a stool at a small table to the side of the stage. I saw her there occasionally, hers being the only face to delineate itself against the mist. It vaguely reassured me, because it was a symbol of past security, and I played on. Then another face appeared beside her: Corinne. What's she doing here? At first, her face jarred discordantly on the landscape, but then the mist adapted her into a darkly resonant minor chord in all its sorrow and beauty.

God, it felt good to be playing again. For the first time in ages, I was able to unwind. I'd forgotten that it was possible to escape so completely from everything, just by concentrating on the music. I could feel Corinne and all her problems melting away, as if they didn't belong to this world, as if they weren't real.

The session drew to a close. Feeling some confusion at Corinne's presence, I approached their table through the thick grey smokiness that was losing its glamour. Hannah pulled out a torn velvet stool she had kept for me.

'That was great, Merle, it really was,' she said enthusiastically.

I smiled uneasily. 'How did you know to come?' I asked Corinne. It was the first time I'd spoken to her since the night of the phone call last week.

She looked anxiously at Hannah. 'I asked Hannah what you were up to, and she told me, so I thought it might be nice to come along.'

'Did you know she was coming?' I asked Hannah, angry at the thought that she'd kept this from me after I'd told her what the state of play was between me and Corinne.

'No,' said Hannah, sounding shocked that I'd think that of her. 'It was a big surprise to me too.' And she seemed to mean it alright.

Corinne looked embarrassed. 'Well, I'd no intention of coming at all, and in fact I was late . . . I, I just decided to come at the last minute, some time after you'd left.'

We said no more, because the rest of the band came over then. After discussing how well it went, we packed up and I set off home with Hannah and Corinne. Outside, the stars had retained some of their magic, and maybe it was seeing this that made Corinne say to me, 'I felt really good tonight – different. It was good for me to come, so I hope you don't mind that I did.' That made some of the tension flow away.

When Hannah's front door had closed behind her for the night, myself and Corinne wandered over to our own. Corinne sat on the doorstep, not wanting to go in yet. It was cool, but not cold. I hovered indecisively with my front door key, wondering whether I should go in or not, but then Corinne asked me to stay out and talk to her for a while.

'There tonight, I felt real bad about that phone call and stuff,' she told me, nervous and apologetic. 'It was strange, because I couldn't make myself feel bad about it up till now. Before I rang him that night, I was asking myself things like "Is this phone call going to work?" and "Is this a mean thing to do?" but I wasn't able to give myself any feelings or judgements about it at all. It was like, something I just had to do.'

'Thanks a lot,' I said sarcastically, feeling a new hardness in the night. 'What made you change your mind?'

'It was the music, I think. Or maybe it was because it was you that was playing – or maybe it was the two of them together. Something, whatever it was, made me feel that I shouldn't have rung him.'

Half-softening, half-reluctant, I sat down beside her.

'Did it make you know why you did it?' I asked.

'No,' she said. 'In fact, I just see it all in the distance, as if it was a scene from a film I saw years ago.'

'What film?' I asked, staring at the clear, distant stars in the sky.

'No film in particular, I didn't mean it like that. I just meant, you know, any old film that you've forgotten. It doesn't mean anything to you and you've forgotten what happened in it, but some vague shadows of it are still there in your memory somewhere.'

There was a strong, double force working here. On the one hand, she was reaching out to me, and I was responding, because she had come out to see the band, and everything she had said about the experience seemed genuine. On the other hand, I got the impression that she was holding her distance, that she was explaining only what suited her. I was inclined to keep my distance too, because I was afraid of her doing something like making another phone call when her mood changed. I think she picked up on how I felt.

'Can we not just put it all behind us?' she asked desperately. 'Come on, you haven't been talking to me for days, and if this goes on any longer, I'll feel totally shut out. I'll probably start falling to pieces again, but I won't let myself, I'll try and put pressure on myself not to.'

'You'll feel shut out?' I said to her. 'Corinne, you never tell me anything, and what you do say I don't understand, or else it turns out to be a lie. Rob probably knows more about you than I do, and I wouldn't even know that, only I saw you together when you were supposed to hate him so much that you came rushing home wanting to keep me away from him.'

'It's not like that, honestly,' she said, panicking. 'I mean everything I say when I say it, and if you don't understand it, well, I don't even understand it myself. I'm trying to explain it to myself as much as I am to you. And I did hate Rob when I told you I did. I don't know why I went to see him and reacted like I did. I just did.'

'Oh, come on, Corinne,' I said, angry at her for appealing to me like this and making me want to believe her against my better judgement. 'What did you mean when you told me I should just accept all that without asking any more questions? And what about Shane? Why did Rob hide his address? Why did the two of you go so odd about him?'

'I don't know,' she said, with what appeared to be genuine regret. 'I don't know any of these things. I wish I did, but I don't.'

As soon as she said that, I dearly wanted to believe her. I didn't, but I thought that if I accepted what she said, then things would be a lot easier. It was impossible to live in the same house, to even sit in the same room, with Corinne while things were the way they were. And I really wanted to be at ease with her, to be at ease in that house where we shared a lifetime of memories, a lifetime of having grown up together.

'I saw Shane a few days ago,' I said. 'He tells me that nothing happened between you, either recently or when you were younger. And the thing is, I believe him and I don't believe him.'

She didn't answer. She didn't even look at me. I sighed.

'Hannah thinks you wanted to kill yourself because of your boyfriend,' I said. 'I told her that had nothing to do with it, but I was thinking afterwards that you were always a bit strange about boyfriends. Do you even know why that was?'

That was easier, she said. She knew that. Even the thought of relationships had always depressed her. She could only explain it in terms of the boyfriend she had when she was fifteen: it was dishonest, she said. It was dishonest for her to go out with him, because she was just doing what she thought she should be doing in the hope that it would fit. But it never did, so she never felt right about it. And the annoying thing was it seemed to fit for everybody else she knew. So of course she left all that behind her, for something more . . . honest.

This was where the stars blackened for me, because I knew

Corinne was talking about her 'friends'. I wondered for the first time whether Rob and Shane had ever hung around with that crowd. No, it was unlikely. Very unlikely.

What was it you liked so much about those 'friends', I asked her. She said that she loved being with people like that at first. You could do whatever you liked whenever you liked, and that was so much better than being restless and bored. She shagged so many of them – they all did. And she was happy with herself, felt that she was making the most of her life. They all talked about living on the edge, and she felt that – some sort of romantic melancholy where you were constantly snatching small pieces of life and pleasure from darkness. So whatever sadness she was prone to, she could both relieve and justify. That was how it felt.

She told me there were never any false pretences. Nobody pretended to care about you when they didn't. That's what she liked about it. She was way more frightened of the proper teenage romance – which was what she got at fifteen – where you got given little love heart jewellery and everything was meant to be great. But it was awful really, because you knew all the time it wasn't the real you the other one wanted.

Oh, she was happy with her 'friends'. So she panicked when she started losing the feeling she had for them. The disillusionment came to a head one night, about a year after she started college. It happened while she was queueing in the toilets of some place where some band was playing. There were two girls standing in front of her, hysterically talking about the fellas in the band – one girl was going for the singer, the other for the guitarist. And in one of the toilets there was a girl crying because the singer had let her down, and even though her friends were with her, you could see that they were sick of her at this stage and didn't care.

'And I just felt so lonely,' says Corinne. 'I didn't know what I was doing there, because the whole thing was just making me feel so alone now. And as I stood there, listening to that girl crying, looking all around me, I couldn't avoid the conclusion that I shouldn't be there at all. There was a very strong light bulb hanging from the ceiling of those toilets, and that bulb showed up everything: the cracked mirrors, the faded graffiti on the wall . . . it even showed me up to myself, making me realize that this scene didn't work for me anymore. And it wasn't as if I had nowhere else to go, but still. I wanted it all to feel as good as it used to, but it didn't.'

'And did you, did you ever get that good feeling back again?' I wanted to know.

'No. I never got that excitement, ever again. Now I wonder if I imagined a lot of it, because it can't have been that good really. I mean, look what happened when I brought you to that party. I don't know how I could have been so stupid as to bring you with me that night. And I don't know what I was thinking of, ringing your man last week. The thought of it makes me sick now, I don't know what I was trying to do. I'd spit on one of them now. I knew they were bastards the whole time I was hanging around with them. I knew they fucked up a lot of girls, and sometimes each other as well. But I didn't care.'

'Why? How could you not have cared?' I asked her.

'I reckoned a lot of them girls would get fucked up anyway, which may sound callous, but the world was like that to me.'

'Why, what could have happened to you that would have touched you deeper than it did me?'

'I don't know, I honestly don't. I know you're still thinking about Rob and Shane, but I was just like that, honestly. Merle, do you remember that day, when you asked me why I wanted to die, and I started going on about how I couldn't feel anything? Well, that was all true, but even still, I don't know if that's why I tried to kill myself. You see, I didn't even think through what my reasons were. I just went ahead and did it because I was too depressed to take any more.'

She stopped there. All that she felt she had to say had been said. But I was still as confused as ever and wanted to know more, wanted to know what exactly she felt about the fella from the party, why she felt she had to ring him last week, and why she regretted it now. But I didn't ask her about any of that. Or tell her, for the first time, about what had happened to me with that other 'friend' after that gig she brought me to when I was fourteen. A stillness had fallen over the night, and it didn't seem right to break it.

'Well, what do you want me to do then?' I asked.

'I don't know. Just, just believe what I say, even if it sounds wrong and contradictory, and, don't hassle me about everything,' said Corinne.

The stars were still black, but at least I could now see them starting to glow through the dark uneasy stillness.

'Well, if you want me to do that, then you have to promise me not to do anything weird or frightening. I won't care what odd things you say, as long as you don't do anything freaky, like ringing your man, or doing stupid things in Rob's flat, or trying to kill yourself. OK?' I asked, nervous and worried about the commitment I was making.

'Oh, you don't have to worry about that. I'm not going to die now, and I only did the other things because I was reacting against you hassling me about that party.'

'But I don't see how you could have reacted so badly, Corinne. I was only talking about what happened to me at a party and asking you about Rob and Shane.'

She stood up. 'It's getting cold now, let's go in. Look, just take my word for it, I don't know exactly why I did all that, but I won't do anything else if you leave me alone.'

I stared at her doubtfully in the shadow of the open door.

166

'OK, Corinne. I won't say another word. Not unless you go and do some other stupid thing.'

Eighteen

Things were quiet for the rest of that week. Corinne had retreated into herself and didn't say much, despite the fact that she spent hours in my room listening to me practise. She was very restless, and couldn't keep still for a minute. But even though she kept pacing up and down whatever room she was in, she told me, when I asked her, that she didn't want to go out for a walk. I hung around the house when I wasn't at work, wanting to keep an eye on her, but she seemed to be alright, so I decided to stop worrying.

I hadn't had much of a chance to talk to Hannah, but I rang her on Friday evening before I went to work, and we arranged to go out the following night. She told me to meet up with her in town, and when I asked her what she would be doing beforehand, she hesitated before telling me that she was going to call in on Shane and Mr Johnson in the late afternoon.

'I see,' I said. 'They mightn't be there though, on a Saturday.'

'They will – I was talking to them a minute ago on the phone. Mr Johnson was saying that he hates going anywhere on a Saturday, what with the crowds and all.'

'Then what was he doing going out the Saturday night Corinne saw them?' I asked sceptically.

'Well, I don't know. He was talking about the day, anyway. Honest to God, Merle,' she said, exasperated.

'Yeah, OK, well, enjoy yourself,' I told her.

It was dark when I left work. But I had to wait only ten minutes for a bus, standing outside the shops where smoky orange street lights burnt away patches of the heavy black sky. The night was very mild, almost like spring – though with none of its freshness or vitality. Fallen leaves, still holding the gloss and texture of life, lay around the skinny trunks of the few trees.

'I thought it'd be nice to try some place different,' said Hannah when I met her in town. 'Mr Johnson was telling me about this really cool place.'

'It's not the pub we were in looking for Shane?' I asked her.

'No,' she told me, as I followed her through streets that were lit almost as brightly as day.

This pub was just like the one we'd been into looking for Shane. It gleamed with all the cold newness of a recently-opened place, but I'd heard of it before, so I knew that it had been there for several years. It was really crowded inside, so we couldn't take a good look around, but at least we hadn't had to queue to get in. Eventually, I managed to get served at the bar, and I squeezed my way back with our drinks to where Hannah was guarding a tiny space on a ledge for us.

'There are some blokes Mr Johnson's age here, but not many,' I said, looking around at the mainly twenty-something crowd as I lit up a smoke. 'Still, he seems to like this age group, doesn't he?'

Hannah took a cigarette out of my box – she usually smoked only when she went out, so she never had any of her own. 'Well, Mr Johnson was saying that he makes sure to bring Shane out to nice places like this sometimes,' she said. 'You wouldn't believe how good he is to Shane, Merle.'

'Oh, very good,' I said. 'I mean, what would a fat bloke his age want with someone young and good-looking like Shane?'

'Now that's not fair, and you know it,' she said angrily. 'Mr

Johnson's turned Shane's life around completely in the last year, taking him in off the streets, giving him a future, the security of a relationship, the strength to give up the drugs . . .'

I had to laugh at that. 'Come off it, Hannah. You make him sound like Mother Teresa or something. I mean, the bloke took total advantage of Shane, because, let's face it, there's no way Shane would have looked twice at him if he hadn't been so vulnerable.'

'Vulnerable?' she stared at me. 'Where did you get that idea?'

'Hannah, he was a young drug addict with no family, no friends, no money. Of course he was vulnerable. And then someone like Mr Johnson comes along, and even though he's a bit of a prick, a total control freak and not very attractive, Shane's so grateful for his attention that it's easy for him to take Shane over.'

She thought about this for a minute, even though she obviously didn't agree with me. 'Yes, well, I don't think so,' she said eventually. 'First of all, Mr Johnson's very nice. You just don't like him because he wouldn't let you pester Shane that day. Second of all, you know as well as I do that Shane used to be such an absolute nightmare that he just made enemies of everyone. Now, I know my parents aren't the most sympathetic people in the world, but even still, they did try, Merle, so if Mr Johnson could get through to him when they couldn't, well then . . .'

'But it's not that simple though, is it?' I said, cutting in on her. 'I mean, it's one thing rejecting your parents and running off when you're sixteen, but it's quite another thing five years later, when you're alone and desperate and this bloke comes along . . .'

'Yeah, maybe, but so what?' Hannah insisted. 'I mean, as long as they're happy . . . That's the main thing, isn't it?'

'Well, Mr Johnson's obviously happy, but what about Shane?' I asked. 'I mean, he can't like being pushed around like that and told what to do all the time. And what's going to happen when Mr Johnson gets bored with him? And if he doesn't, well, what's going to happen when Mr Johnson gets a bit older? I mean the bloke must be at least thirty years older than Shane, and let's face it, it's no love affair, is it?'

'That's not fair of you, Merle,' said Hannah, angry again. 'Honestly, if you had just seen them together this afternoon, you wouldn't be talking like this.'

'Yeah, OK, maybe,' I said, seeing no point in pissing her off. 'So what were they saying to you, anyway?'

'Oh, we were just chatting about this and that,' she said. 'Mr Johnson was telling me that he used to be a dentist.'

'A dentist!' The thought of it was so funny that I nearly choked on my pint. 'Oh my God. Imagine going to him to get your teeth filled!'

'I'm glad you think it's funny,' she said, looking at me. 'He says it's the most boring job in the world, and that he got so sick of filling teeth that he had to sell his practice, take early retirement, and move to Ireland.'

'Unfortunately for us,' I remarked, finishing my drink.

'Merle!' said Hannah, annoyed.

'Sorry. Are you ready for another one?' I asked, looking at her empty glass. Honestly, though, a *dentist*?

If anything, the pub was more crowded now than it had been when we came in, with throngs of people gathered around the bar, jostling for service. But by the time I got back from the bar, Hannah had managed to secure two high stools near where we had been standing.

'Nice one,' I said, depositing our pints on the ledge. 'I was dying to sit down.'

'Yeah, so was I,' she agreed, taking her drink.

'So Mr Johnson must have made a lot of money,' I speculated.

'Yeah, he said the money's good alright,' Hannah agreed.

171

'Still though, a house like that must have cost an absolute bomb,' I commented.

'Oh, yeah. He was saying that it was very expensive, and that he had to spend a fortune doing it up. But he got a good price for the place he had in America, and as well as that, his mother died a few years ago and he had the money he got from selling her house, so . . .'

'Well for some,' I said, lighting up again. 'God, you know a lot about him.'

'No, not really, just what he was telling me,' she said.

'And what made him decide to come to Ireland?' I asked her.

'He said his family were Irish originally, so he liked the idea of getting in touch with his roots, or whatever. But as well as that, he wanted to retire somewhere smaller and quieter than where he was from.'

'Oh right. Where's he from?' I wondered.

'I don't know, actually. He didn't say,' she said.

'And you didn't ask him?'

'Well, like, he was doing most of the talking,' she said defensively. I could imagine it alright. Him controlling the conversation as usual.

'I see. Well, he must be from somewhere big if he thinks Dublin's quiet,' I said, looking around the overcrowded pub. 'But I thought he said he hated the crowds in town.'

'He does, but he says it's not too bad during the week. And besides, there's some nice pubs and restaurants where he lives.'

'So, what with the night-life and the young men, Dublin's one big party,' I said.

'Is he not allowed to enjoy himself?' Hannah asked crossly.

'It's a free country, isn't it?' I retorted. 'So, would many Americans come to live here, then?'

'Oh, you'd be surprised,' she said. 'Mr Johnson says there's a lot of them around, but he wouldn't know them – he keeps himself to himself.'

You mean he keeps Shane to himself, I thought, but I didn't say it.

'Were you with them long?' I asked her.

'About two hours or so,' she told me. 'I got the bus over there when I was finished going round the shops.'

'Oh yeah, what did you buy?' I asked, remembering the plastic bag I'd seen her carrying.

She took the bag out from under her jacket, which she'd pushed into the corner of our ledge, and she handed me a slinky black top, taking care to keep it away from our drinks and the ashtray.

'Very nice,' I said, opening it out. 'How much was it?' I asked, turning over the price tag.

'Thirty,' she said. 'Which wasn't bad at all, considering where I got it.'

'No,' I agreed. 'God, I must go shopping myself. I haven't been into the shops in ages, and I really need to get a few things.'

'You see, you've been too busy worrying about Corinne to get anything done,' she said, shaking a finger at me. 'How is she, anyway?'

'Oh, she seems to be alright,' I said. 'A bit quiet, though.'

'You wouldn't mind that,' said Hannah. 'Did she enjoy the other night?'

'She did, yeah. I'm glad she came.'

'Yeah, me too. And I thought she seemed a lot better, so maybe the two of you can just put all this behind you and get on with it.'

'Yeah, maybe,' I said, not wanting to speculate any further. We finished our pints and left soon afterwards, so tired that we nearly fell asleep on the bus.

Nineteen

I was in really good form after that Saturday night. And even though Corinne was still kind of quiet, I didn't worry about her. Not even when she said she was too tired to come to the Tuesday night gig.

'How can you be tired from doing nothing?' I asked her.

She shrugged her shoulders from where she was sitting, opposite the television. 'I just am,' she said. 'And I want to watch telly.'

'Sure what's on on a Tuesday night?' I wanted to know.

'Oh, there'll be something on,' she said, flicking through the channels.

So I left her there. I had a good night, and I didn't worry about her. In fact, all was quiet until the vicious storm that closed in around the house on Thursday, loudly shaking and pushing the walls in on us. Then the lights went dead on Thursday night while I was arranging on the phone in the hall to go to band practice the following night.

'I have to go,' I told the band, wondering if it was just the lights that had gone.

'OK. You're sure you can come tomorrow night?' they asked me, because they were ringing from a phone box – their phone had been cut off because they hadn't paid the bill and I wouldn't be talking to them after this, so I had to let them know now whether I was coming or not.

'Oh yeah, it's no problem' I said, watching Mam come into the hall with a torch.

It was a full-scale power cut. Mam of course had boxes of candles put away for emergencies like this and she had already given some to Corinne. Now she handed me a box before going across the road to give some to a friend.

I shone my way through the dark up to Corinne's room to see what she was up to. She was sitting on the floor, leaning over a candle. It took me a few seconds to realize that she was burning her right wrist.

'Corinne!' I screamed at her. 'What are you doing?'

She looked at me with absolute confusion, almost as if she didn't recognize me, or couldn't quite place me in the room. There were tears in her eyes, but she didn't stop. So I pulled her hand away from the searing flame and placed the two candles well away from her.

'What's wrong with you Corinne? You said you wouldn't do any more of this stuff!'

I sat down beside her in shock, not knowing what to do. The rain cried down on the window with a frightening intensity and the shaken, unsteady candles cast flickering, distorted shadows across the room, transforming it into something liquid and grotesque.

'It's the candles. I thought the pain would make them go away,' said Corinne, all worked up into a state of panic and terror.

I didn't understand her. A panic of my own grabbed me in the dimness of the room because I couldn't understand her and I didn't know what to do.

'Just blow them out then, if they're disturbing you,' I whispered.

'No, no, that's worse. I can't be in the dark after candles, I just see worse images,' she said, terrified.

I tried to control my panic, stared at her, trying to get a handle on this, to relate this to what she'd done before. It was difficult, with the room shaking under the pressure of the weather and Corinne shaking at the sight of two small candles, but I tried. I remembered that day in the pub when she tried to explain why she wanted to die and how, when she tried to describe the effect Shane had had on her, she said, 'This is how I felt,' and held her finger into a lighter. But that was different. That was less . . . extreme. Still, though, it was the same thing, wasn't it? I need it to be the same thing. I need to understand.

'What do the candles make you see, Corinne?' I asked quietly, afraid that even the sound of my voice might set her off again.

'I don't know. It's just, it's just something horrible,' she whispered, distressed.

'Come on, Corinne, try and tell me what it is.'

'I don't want to. I'm telling you, it's not nice. You don't want to know.' She was angry now.

'Fucking right I do,' I said. 'I promised you I'd leave you alone if you didn't do anything like this again, but look at you, Corinne! You have to let me help you, or, or at least if you want me to leave you alone in future, then you'll have to explain what you're thinking, and what it is you're seeing so that I'll understand why you're like this and why I'm to leave you alone.'

She looked at me with hostility, and as if it was a real effort for her to focus her thoughts. But then some awareness of how she was hurting me and some effort to communicate how sorry she was for this passed over her face.

'Look, I'm not really sure what I'm thinking,' she said eventually. 'It's just, I'm in a room, with candles, and it's making me feel terrible.' She started to shudder even more.

'OK, why is it worse when the candles go out?' I was almost afraid to ask, but I persisted all the same.

'Because whatever's happening gets worse.' She pulled and scraped at her face in distress. Trickles of blood surged to the surface. 'And that's all I can tell you, right?'

'OK, OK, just tell me this then, are you on your own?' I asked, seeing as I'd gotten this far.

'I don't know. No, I don't think so.'

I held my breath. 'Are Rob and Shane with you?'

She threw a cushion at me angrily. 'Why did you have to go and say that? It's not enough for me to tell you once that no, they're not there, they're never there! You just keep at me and at me, don't you?'

'Who's there then?' I asked her.

Corinne stood up and stumbled around the room, holding the candle at an awkward angle. 'I don't know, and I don't want to know either. If you just knew what it felt like, you'd understand. Oh God, Merle, I can't go on like this, it's too much for me.'

Can't go on like this. Does she mean the way she feels tonight, or the way she's been feeling ever since she saw Shane that night? Or does she mean the way she's been feeling all her life? Does this mean that everything I've done to unlock the reasons behind her wanting to kill herself is wasted because she's going to die anyway? She was burning her wrist again.

'Corinne, take your hand out, please!'

She stared at me, bewildered. 'But if I can't do that, then I'll have to do this.' And she set one of the curtains on fire.

I don't think I ever moved as fast in my life. That's how I managed to put the flames out quickly with the other curtain.

'For fuck sake, Corinne! What are you at?' I asked furiously.

I looked over at her and saw that she was shaking. The burnt smell dominated and deadened the room. I opened the window

177

to dispel it. The wind and rain lashed the remnants of the curtains up and down, giving the darkened room a surreal hue.

'Maybe it's best if I stay away from you, Corinne. I only seem to make you worse.' I was in the pits of despair.

'No!' she begged. 'You can't leave me on my own! I told you before that you were the only one I could talk to, and I meant it.'

Her words are desperate, but there's something in the way she says them that almost doesn't ring true, and it's disturbing. All the more so when I tried to figure out where all this came from and where it was going, and whether it was better or worse if it didn't get there. I pulled the table and chair away from the open window so that the rain wouldn't destroy them and drew the burnt curtains to protect the walls and carpet. Then I went to leave the room. Corinne called me back from the door.

'Merle, I can't stay here tonight with the smell. Can I sleep on your floor? Please?'

So I let my very disturbed sister into my room. I don't know that either of us slept. I lay there the whole time, listening to the onslaught of the weather, too conscious of Corinne's presence to even breathe properly.

Twenty

The wind and rain continued to darken and enclose the house the following day. I used the weather as an excuse to wander around the house, telling Mam it was too rotten to go to college when it must have been obvious to her that I hadn't gone in weeks. She wasn't even worried about Corinne – we told her that the curtain had been set on fire accidentally by the candle and that Corinne had burnt her hand trying to put the fire out. And she thought Corinne was asleep all day trying to recover from that. She didn't even think it was odd that Corinne had refused to move from my floor into a bed this morning and was still lying there, drifting in and out of a restless sleep.

I got ready around six to go to band practice. Thankfully the rain had stopped for the time being, though the wind was loud and harsh. Still, at least I wasn't going to get wet on my way over there, though I had decided to leave my guitar at home and use their spare one, because I wasn't taking any chances in this weather.

It was only when I was about to leave that Corinne made an appearance downstairs, not even dressed. She looked terrible, and I felt guilty for not having the time to talk to her. I tried to ignore this though, remembering how such intense talking, which built up the pressure to exploding point, had been going on for ages, and it never got us very far. If anything, I only made her worse.

'Well, I'll see you later then, OK?' I told her.

She didn't say anything, but she looked weird, weirder than usual. I opened the door, but I continued to hover anxiously for a few minutes.

'You will be alright, won't you?' I asked her. 'You won't go and burn the house down or anything while I'm gone?'

She bit her lip. 'It looks like it's going to start raining again soon, so I wouldn't be able to do much damage, would I?' She sounded quite serious, and I was on the verge of considering staying in. But she pushed me out the door, saying, 'Go on, I'm not going to do anything. I'll just get some food and watch telly.'

Outside, the wind relentlessly pulled and tore at everything, and it was all I could do to resist being swept off the path and into the middle of the road. Nevertheless, I managed to get to the bus stop in one piece and I leaned against the bus shelter, thinking about Corinne. Thinking about how she couldn't see or describe anything last night apart from being able to say that she was in a room with a candle. And I remembered how she once confused some image with her memory of that bloody party, and how once before that, she associated the image of a middle-aged drunk with a dodgy lane.

Eventually a bus came and I got on, trying to picture her image to myself. This is her: in a room with a candle. If I separate what really happened at the party from her memory of it, then there's probably someone who gave her heavy jewellery in that room as well. But that's as far as I can go with her memory – she may have got the details of the party wrong, but that doesn't mean that something similar happened to her. All I know is that something terrible is happening in a room.

I reached the band's house in a daze. They answered the door, and once I was inside, they told me that their old guitarist had come back. They were mortified, seeing as I'd come all this way in such dreadful weather, but there was no helping it – he's a cousin of one of them and an old friend, and he was meant to be moving to Galway but he came back, so . . .

So there was absolutely no point in my coming all the way over here. Oh well. They told me not to go home right away, to sit down and have a cup of tea or something. But I didn't feel like hanging around, so I left.

At least I don't have a guitar with me, so I can do stuff if I want. I could go home and see how Corinne is, but I'd rather not. Not yet.

I thought about going for a walk, but the sky was heavy with clouds and it was starting to rain again. So I picked my way down the wet pavement, which was all sleek with reflected streetlight and washed brown leaves, some of which clung to the ground in spite of the wind. I headed towards the bus stop and decided to go to the cinema.

I hadn't been to the cinema since the summer. It seemed so long ago now that I couldn't even remember what I'd been to see, except that it had been one afternoon at the end of one of the few weeks of blue skies and burning sunshine and dried-up air. Me and Hannah had grown tired of the heat and turned instead to the comfort of a cold, dark cinema. Tonight, the conditions had been reversed, and it was the cinema that was warm and stuffy with no air.

I was too distracted to focus on the film, except to register that it was set somewhere in America with stunning beaches and that the characters all had amazing cars and amazing clothes. One of them looked a lot like Shane, only he was a bit more confident and probably a lot less screwed-up. The screen blurred into a bright dazzle before me as I replayed last night for about the millionth time. Jesus Christ, how deranged can you get? What kind of nutter tries to burn their house down in order to escape images they can't even see clearly or relate to? Corinne's some mess alright. Who knows what she'll do next.

And the thing is, she's gone to such an extreme that I can't even begin to understand what must be going on in her head. It's almost as if whatever's been disturbing her from the time she tried to kill herself has taken on a life of its own and swallowed her up completely. I don't even know that girl anymore. In fact, I feel as if I've lost the threads of any ideas I might have had about where she went wrong. All my theories about Shane and Mr Johnson in the pub, about Rob, and about shit that might have happened when Corinne and them were sixteen, are all insubstantial figments of my imagination compared with the impact last night had on me. Fuck. I can almost feel my wrist burning the way hers was. And I can still smell the way the burnt curtains stank up the room. And I can feel the way the wind and rain flooded the room in cold, bitter waves when I opened the window. But last night's so vivid in my mind, and it's taken on such unnatural proportions that I begin to half-believe it hasn't happened at all. And how can you worry about what hasn't happened?

God, this was such a cop-out, but I was so tired I decided to just leave things the way they were for the moment. Yeah, I was worried alright, but now what I needed was some sleep. So I left the cinema about half an hour before the end and headed home.

When I got back to the house, Corinne had already gone to bed, in her room this time. That's something, anyway, I thought, remembering how scared she'd been to sleep there last night. I rang Hannah, wanting to arrange to meet her the following night, which was Saturday, but she wasn't there. Maybe it was just as well – I could barely keep my eyes open, never mind talk to someone, and I didn't stay up much longer after that.

Twenty-one

When I woke up the following morning, the wind had slackened just a bit and the sky was a lighter shade of grey. Even so, the rain continued to fall and the weather was almost as rotten as it had been the last two days. Corinne wasn't up yet, but that wasn't surprising, seeing as it was early. I wouldn't have got up myself if I hadn't had to go to work. But I decided to ring Hannah anyway, because she was usually up around now. When I asked her where she'd been last night, she said she'd been to see Shane and Mr Johnson again.

'Oh yeah?' I said. 'How's Shane?'

'Oh, he seems to be in great form,' she answered.

'That's good,' I said. 'What about that Mr Johnson?'

'I know you find this hard to believe,' she said, 'but I actually like him. I'm actually grateful for all he's done for Shane, so I enjoy going to see him.'

'Did you tell your mam where you were?' I asked her.

'What do you think?'

'Yeah, I know, but does she not wonder where you are?'

'She just thinks I'm out with new friends from college,' she said. 'Anyway, what are we doing tonight?'

'We're going out,' I said. 'I'm absolutely wrecked, so I shouldn't be going anywhere, but I can't stay in, because . . .' I looked around to see if anyone else had come downstairs, and when I was sure they hadn't, I said, 'Corinne's gone completely psycho again, and I don't know what to do about her.'

'That's terrible. What's up with her?' Hannah asked, concerned, but not surprised.

'I'll tell you later.'

'OK,' she said. 'And I have stuff to tell you too.'

I was so tired in work that it was a miracle I got through the day at all. After I'd given the wrong change about three times, I started counting out people's money as slowly as possible so as not to make any more mistakes. Everyone was looking at me, wondering if I'd left my brain at home. But at least I finished up early that day, so I had time to go home, get some food and get changed before heading out again. I asked Corinne if she wanted to come, but I was glad when she said she couldn't be arsed going anywhere. I knew that Mam was having some friends over, so I reckoned that Corinne couldn't come to much harm with all them in the house. Anyway, it was getting late, so I called for Hannah and we set off into the stormy night, hurrying down to the bus stop so that we wouldn't get too wet.

In town, the crowds were slightly less dense than usual, probably due to the weather. We tried two full pubs, including the one we used to go to every week, before ending up in the one we'd been in last Saturday night, where we actually managed to get two stools almost right off.

'So what's been happening with Corinne?' Hannah asked once we were settled.

'You don't want to know,' I answered. But I needed to talk to someone about it, so I told her anyway.

'Oh my God,' she said softly, and then fell silent for a while.

I smoked one cigarette in the dim light and couldn't help but overhear some of the conversation of a loud group whose backs were almost pressing into us. They were all out for someone's birthday, and they seemed to be having a great time. I knew it was unlikely that they'd ever be quiet enough to hear what *we* were saying, but I wondered what they'd think of us if they did. Oh well.

'It's impossible to know what to think, really,' said Hannah eventually. 'I mean, I can't but believe there's something in your theory. But at the same time, I really do believe Mr Johnson and Shane when they tell me that nothing happened that night. I mean, I've spent a good bit of time with them now, so I think I'd know if they were having me on.'

'Maybe,' I said, not altogether sure about that. 'But is it Shane or Mr Johnson that does all the talking?'

'Meaning?'

'Well, Mr Johnson'd be the kind of person that'd only tell you what suited him, so I wouldn't pass much heed of what he says.'

'Honest to God, Merle, you'd think he was some kind of monster the way you go on! I mean, so what if he's a bit protective of Shane. Wouldn't you be the same if you were in his shoes? And besides, Mr Johnson's had a rough time of it these past few years, so he deserves to be left in peace.'

'Him have a rough time of it?' I asked, both sceptical and curious.

'Oh yes,' she said. 'It just came out by accident there last night, when we were chatting away. I was saying that my boss at work had just started golf or something, and then Mr Johnson said that this boyfriend of his used to play a lot of golf back in the States. So I asked him how come he stopped playing it, and Mr Johnson told me that he was dead. So I said I was sorry to hear that, and I asked him were they very close, and he said they'd been together for ten years, right up until he died.'

'What did he die of?'

'Cancer,' she told me. 'Mr Johnson said it was such a horrible way to die. And he was so lonely and depressed afterwards that it was then he decided to get out of his job and make a fresh start of it in Ireland.'

'God,' I said. 'And then he came here and found Shane,' I added.

'Yeah, I think that's nice,' said Hannah.

Nice for him anyway, whatever about Shane.

'Well, I'm sure there's a lot about Shane that he doesn't know,' I said. 'And I'm pretty sure now that whatever Corinne's upset about happened long before she saw the two of them together in that pub. But if that's the case, then I don't understand why she got so disturbed when she did see them.'

'True. Oh, I don't know what you're going to do, Merle.'

'Neither do I,' I said. 'And who knows what Corinne's up to right now while we're sitting here talking about her.'

'I wouldn't worry about it too much,' said Hannah. 'You've done all you can for her, so come on, let's talk about something else. Did you go to band practice last night?'

'Oh yeah,' I said. 'They kicked me out.'

'They didn't! And after you were so good, learning all their songs at such short notice. The cheek of them!'

'I'm not too bothered about it,' I said. 'What happened was their old guitarist decided he wanted to stay in Dublin after all, so . . .'

'So you're out. Oh well, maybe you'll have time to come to college now.'

'Oh, no. I couldn't face having to sit through hours of that stuff – there's too much on my mind,' I explained. 'Speaking of college though, have you seen Danielle lately?'

'No. Did I tell you I tried ringing her? Anyway, I left a few messages, but she never got back to me.'

'Who answered the phone on you?' I asked, wondering if she'd been talking to Rob.

'Oh, I don't know who they were,' she said. 'It wasn't Rob,

anyway. God, I'd love to know if they're still going out, after what happened with Corinne.'

'So would I.'

'Actually,' said Hannah. 'I finish work at around three tomorrow, so I might give her a ring then, and if she's around, I'll go straight over there. Do you want to come?'

'No, I'd better not, seeing as she probably hates my guts.'

'Oh, I'm sure she doesn't. It wasn't your fault what happened. Anyway, I'll sort all that out for you, so don't worry about it.'

Hannah had to be up early in the morning, so we left soon afterwards. Outside, the wind howled as ferociously as ever, and the rain was way heavier than it had been. Walking down the street was like wading through a city that had half-sunk into the sea. But we managed to get home in one piece.

Twenty-two

I woke up around two o'clock the next day. I thought I was still tired and I tried to go back to sleep, but I felt so hot I had to wake up.

'Why is it so warm in here?' I asked Mam when I went downstairs.

'Oh, Corinne was saying she was cold the last couple of days, so I've had the heating on high all the time. Of course, now that the house is finally nice and warm, she takes it into her head that she has to go out and do a few things.'

I looked out the window. The light had been pretty much sucked out of the sky, so it might as well have been night-time. And it was raining. It was easily the worst day so far this week.

'Oh yeah? Where did she go?' I asked.

'To see some friends, I think.'

What friends? I went upstairs and sat in my room, wondering if I should be worried or not, but I couldn't make up my mind. I even went and stood in Corinne's doorway, remembering Thursday night. Who knows where she is or what she's doing. Oh, go and ring Hannah and see what she thinks, I decided. At this stage, I can't tell if I'm over-reacting or not, so it'd be as well to get someone else's perspective on this. So I went into my mam's room, closed the door, and rang Hannah. But she wasn't there. Oh yeah, I remembered. She was working until three and then she was going to ring Danielle and go over to see her if she was there. Well, it's nearly half-three now, so she could well be on her way over there. I decided to ring Danielle to see what the story was. Is that a good idea, though? Would she not be pissed off with me, seeing as I'm Corinne's sister? Oh, fuck it. I was getting so impatient now that I had to do something, so I picked up the phone and dialled the number, even though it had also occurred to me that Rob might answer it. But he didn't. Danielle did. Her tone went neutral when she found out it was me.

'Is Hannah with you?' I asked.

'No. She rang earlier from work to say she was coming over, alright, but then she rang back to say she had to stay late at work, so she won't be over now.'

'Oh right,' I said, disappointed. 'So how are you, anyway?'

'Well, I've been better. And yourself?'

'Oh, fine, I suppose.' Then I thought I might as well. 'And how's Rob?'

'Why don't you ask your sister that?' she said.

'Oh, Danielle, I'm really sorry about what happened that day. Honestly, I . . .'

'Oh, I'm not talking about that,' she said. 'I'm talking about right now, this minute. She's been up there with him for the last hour and a half.'

'No way,' I said, worried.

So he was the friend she'd gone to see. Oh God. And the last time she got weird, she went to see him too. Something told me I'd better get over there right away. Should I ask Danielle to tell them I was coming? No, I don't want to set Corinne off into doing something stupid if she's there. And besides, Rob was kind of odd himself the time I saw him with her, so it's better to be safe than sorry. But maybe I could get Danielle to keep an eye on them without getting into all this.

'And are you not up there with them?' I asked.

'No, I'm kind of fighting with Rob. He's being a real prick to me, as usual.'

'Are you going to break it off with him then?'

'Oh I don't know.' She sounded pissed off. 'I think about it sometimes, but I still like him, you know?'

I knew alright. I'd heard it all before. 'Well, look, could you do me a favour then? I'm going to come over there now, because I'm really worried about Corinne and I need to talk to her right away, so could you go in to them or something and make sure they don't go out before I get there? But whatever you do, don't tell them I'm coming over.'

'Why not?' she asked, sensing something was up. 'And why are you worried about her?'

'Oh, it's a long story, and I'll tell you about it some other time. Just don't tell her I'm coming, OK?'

I grabbed my jacket and told Mam I was going out.

'You're going out too?' she said. 'On a day like this? You'll both catch your death of cold.'

Outside, the wind and rain pounded down, flooding the kerbs. The wind blew everyone's umbrellas backwards and broke them. Everyone rushed along, not looking where they were going, but I didn't feel them banging into me. I was so busy trying to figure out what was happening that I was untouched by the rain, no matter how much I dripped and got soaked. Luckily, I wasn't waiting long for a bus, but the bad weather made the traffic slower than ever, and it seemed an eternity before I was thrown up on to Rob's road. The place looked as trapped and warped as ever. I walked slowly towards the weather-bashed door and rang Danielle's bell. She answered grimly, letting me into the harshly-lit hall.

'They're not here,' she said sulkily.

'What do you mean they're not here?' I asked, panicking.

'They went out just after you rang,' she told me.

'And, and . . . did you not stop them?'

'No,' she said. 'I went up to them alright, and just as I was going in, I heard them talking about going to the park. I would have tried to stop them, only Rob was so ignorant to me.'

'Why, what did he say to you?' I asked, my mind on the park and what they were doing there. Not the sort of place you'd think of going on a day like this.

'Oh, he looked really pissed off when he saw me and said, "So, what's the story with you then?" meaning "What the fuck are you doing here?" Then he said, "We're going out now, bye," and fucked off without even saying where they were going or asking me to go with them.'

'Where's the park?' I said, cutting in on her.

Scowling, she told me, and asked me with some vindictiveness to tell her later exactly what I interrupted. I opened the front door without answering her. She called me back.

'What do you think I should do?' she asked.

'About what?' I was in a hurry to be gone.

'About Rob of course.'

It wasn't her fault, but I was about to lose the head with her. 'Oh, we'll talk about it later,' I said and ran off.

The park was still open when I got there, but I didn't hear a sound as I walked through the gates. The storm must have put people off coming here today. I made my way through the tunnels of bare trees, kicking aside the mounds of dead leaves and broken branches, but there was no sign of Rob or Corinne. And the wind and rain created awful noises and shadows, scaring the hell out of me. Finally, I came out beside a large pond and there they were. Oh my God. It looked as if Corinne was lying in the water. But then I realized that she was lying at the very edge of the path, only the water had risen in the rain and was spilling over her on to the path, trying to swallow her. She was talking to Rob, who was sitting further back on the firm, wet path. I was behind them, and they were so engrossed in their conversation that they didn't see me.

'I'm so happy we came here,' she was saying. 'I was getting claustrophobic all the time I was inside. And even outside, I felt that the streets and houses were closing in on me.'

He didn't answer her, but it was like she didn't need him to. It was the same as that day in the flat: there was some kind of bond between them, something that drew them together, making them one of a kind. There was the same tense stillness, the same dark attitude in the way they were fixed in their cold, wet places, unmoved by the pressure of the storm that shook everything around them.

'I could die very happily here,' she said. 'What do you think Rob? They say drowning is the most peaceful way to go, and I can almost feel that peace now, just from lying here. But it's a poisonous peace, because it makes all this park around me turn sour. I can feel some kind of infection spreading all over it, and the only way to escape it is to give myself completely and sink into the peace.'

Jesus Christ. I felt like I'd been hit. So stunned, I couldn't move. I was unable to think about what I was hearing, I could only feel its terrible implications.

'Yeah, I know what you mean,' Rob told her.

'So why not die now then?' asked Corinne.

As the initial shock wore off, I began to hear their voices in all their genuine, ghostlike quality, chilling me completely but also making me feel that I didn't belong here, that I should go away and not interfere, let them take their logic to its end. But because I didn't want them to die, I fought against their need for escape and resolution, and stepped forward. Rob saw me first.

'What are you doing here?' he asked, angry.

Corinne turned her head. 'You just can't leave me alone, can you?' she screamed.

'I couldn't help it, I was worried about you,' I said, recognizing their anger and surprise but desperate to know where the intensity of it came from, seeing as Corinne had been begging me so recently not to walk away from her.

'It's none of your business what she does,' Rob told me.

'And what makes it your business?' I asked him, furious at that.

'Just go away, Merle, please,' Corinne begged me. 'If you care about me at all, just walk away and forget you ever saw us here. If you knew how bad I felt all the time, you wouldn't try to stop me, you'd just let me go.'

An eternity of bewilderment and space passed in a few seconds between her, me, the storm and the dark, creeping water that pulled violently yet soothingly at her. I thought of all the years we had spent together as sisters. There were the early years, when she was simply there all the time. And then there were the clearer, sharper memories of encroaching alienation and separation, caused mainly by what had happened with her 'friends'. Then there was all that had happened recently. But no matter what she did, she had always been there, always, and I had always identified with her above anyone else.

Here she was, pleading with me to let her go, and I felt the force of that need. But I also remembered how she had been that Tuesday night after my gig, pleading with me to accept her, not to push her away, and promising she wasn't going to try to kill herself again. So what does she really want? Is tonight's death wish just a shift in mood brought on by the storm and the park, a mood that might change by morning if only I can stop her from doing this?

And then I remembered how she had told me on Thursday night that she didn't know why she felt so bad. Even if I have to let her go, surely it can't be right for her to go without even knowing what's wrong, without even knowing what those images are that made her want to burn the house and do all the other stuff. And if Corinne's lying and she does know what caused all this, then surely she owes it to me, after all that's passed between us, to tell me what it is.

'Why do you feel so bad, Corinne?' I asked. 'I know you told me the other night that you didn't know, but you must have some idea.'

'Oh God,' she said. 'Why are you still on at me? Don't you think I'd tell you if I knew? Don't you think it's so much worse not to know? Because at least if you knew, then you could blame something, there'd be something concrete for you to throw it on, and you might even be able to do something about it. But like this? It's like, I look at the sun on a summer's day, it shines hard and pleases everybody else, but it shines so hard on me that I feel it bringing the sky down on top of me. I can't hold it up and I suffocate, so I want to die, and I wonder, is it the sun's fault? Then on a night like this, I stand in the black rain. It's cold and miserable, but I find it cleansing and soothing, so I stand and stand. Eventually, the rain gets too heavy as well, it presses me to the ground, and I want to give in to it, I want to die in it. So I wonder, is it the rain's fault? Don't you see, Merle, everything that breathes light and reality and emotion into other people turns to poison when it reaches me. And I just can't live like that anymore, so let me go, *please*.'

Her sadness spread over me like the gloom of the unlit park. A sense of having failed to reach her, and of being on the edge of final, irrevocable darkness.

'And what about you?' I said, turning from the intensity of the haunted Corinne to Rob. 'Do you feel the same as her? Can you even understand what it's like for her?'

'Oh, I know what it's like alright,' he said quietly. 'It's like, like . . .' he searched for the words, 'it's like a dark shadow has hung over me all my life,' he said.

The cloud of impenetrable grey smoke that had always surrounded him had lifted for a moment then fallen back around him, heavier than ever. I wondered if there was any way of lifting it again.

'Are you going to die too?' I asked him.

Rob didn't answer me. He just looked over at Corinne with some confusion and unease. Then he shrugged his shoulders, but instead of expressing ambivalence, they seemed to say yes.

'And how come you two have this in common?' I asked him.

Corinne laughed hysterically from the water. 'Now she's going to start on about Shane again,' she said. 'Oh Merle, what can I do to convince you? You know you're the only one that means anything to me in this life, and I can't leave until I know you understand that I just am what I am and that's why I'm doing this.'

Something in her voice cut me and buried itself in the open wound. But it wasn't like a bullet. It was a harpoon, and, much as the missile hurt, it was the end of a line she had thrown from her to me, and it was a connection that I could hold. She lay there, burning me out with her eyes while I felt the impact of the wound. I felt her pain and my own and that suddenly resolved me on what to do.

'A week ago last Tuesday, I said I'd leave you alone provided you didn't do anything mad,' I reminded her. 'But on Thursday night, you burnt the curtain and tonight you want to die, so I think I've the right to ask you one more thing.'

I paused with a weakening resolve, struggling not to be overcome.

'I want you and Rob to come with me to Shane's now,' I said. 'And I want the three of you to swear to me that nothing ever happened to make you what you are. And if you do, then that's fair enough, and I won't put any more pressure on you. I'll, I'll miss you, but I won't stand in your way.'

An awful silence spread over them. The sharp steel buried itself deeper inside me as I felt Corinne's hold on the line strengthen. The pact simmered and festered under the cold rain until we absorbed it fully. Rob looked very uncomfortable, but there was something so monumental and binding about it that he seemed dumbstruck, even though he was struggling to break the silence.

'It's nearly six now,' I said. 'The park-keeper should be coming around soon enough to close the place up. You don't want him to find you here, do you?'

'Let's go then,' said Corinne, standing up and facing me.

We walked in silence, fighting our way against the forceful wind which seemed intent on driving us back to the water. All the way to the gate, through the furious, flickering tree shadows and the dead, restless leaves that jumped up and hit us. My mind was on fire. What exactly do I think I'm doing? I've been running around in circles these last weeks, asking each of them if anything ever happened to them, and if they said no before, why would they say yes now? And what about Rob? He doesn't owe me one like Corinne does. He's obviously doing this for her sake. But why? Maybe they'll reach breaking point now and tell me. If I'm to believe what they have already told me, then this'll be the first time in years that all three of them are together at the same time, and that might spark off something and make them talk.

But what if it doesn't? And what if it's not enough to change Corinne's mind? I'll have to let my sister die. The anxiety corroded my mind, but there was little I could do. Even if I can stop her this time from killing herself, I won't be able to stop her another time. And besides, to try to stop her would be a betrayal. She'd die holding that against me.

Twenty-three

We reached the gate and walked back towards civilization. As we passed other people, their normality made my brain kick in again, and I became conscious that my clothes were so wet they were sticking to me.

'This is ridiculous,' I said, looking at Rob and Corinne, who were not only soaking wet but filthy, with muck and dead leaves clinging to them from having been lying on the ground. 'We can't go anywhere looking like this. Why don't we put it off until tomorrow or something?'

There were a few moments of silence. I stared up at the sky through the impenetrable barriers of rain. And then back down the road at the park gate, where the captured rain shone up the black metal and flowed off it in sparkling, vibrant streams. It was Corinne who eventually spoke.

'If we're doing this, we're doing it tonight,' she said. 'I don't want to have it hanging over me until tomorrow.' But even as she spoke, I noticed that she was shivering with the cold.

'But you must be starving, Corinne,' I said. 'You can't have had anything to eat all day.'

'So? I can't eat when I'm like this.'

'Speak for yourself,' said Rob. 'As far as I'm concerned, I'm going to the chipper and then I'm going home.'

'Will you come to Shane's with us tomorrow, then?' I asked him.

'I thought you were going to give that one a miss,' he said. 'I am, anyway.'

'But you said you'd come,' I urged him.

'I said I'd go tonight,' he said. 'And you've said yourself that it's not a good idea.'

'Well . . .' I said slowly, trying to find a way around this. 'Why don't we all go home, get changed, get something to eat, and then meet up again?'

'I'm not hanging around waiting for you two to go all the way home and back again,' said Rob.

'OK,' I said. 'Then we'll go back to your place so that you can get changed. And me and Corinne'll just have to hope that Danielle'll lend us some of her clothes.'

'Not bloody likely,' said Rob, but he sullenly started to walk in that direction. Me and Corinne followed him. When we got as far as the shops, he hesitated and then offered to go to the chipper for us if we wanted to go on to Danielle's. Surprised that he was being decent, I gave him money and he headed off. We continued on.

'Let me do the talking,' I told Corinne as we approached the front door. 'Seeing you is just going to get her back up.'

I rang Danielle's doorbell. Her eyes narrowed when she answered the door and saw Corinne standing there beside me.

'Danielle, can I talk to you for a minute?' I asked, pulling her towards the back of the hall and almost tripping over someone's bike in the process. In a low voice, I told her that I'd found the other two in the park in a terrible state, and that I didn't know what to do. Lowering my voice further, I explained that Corinne had tried to kill herself not too long ago and that it had something to do with Rob and this fella Shane. Remember Shane? The one whose address Rob hid and all that. Anyway,

198

the three of us were all going to see Shane now, only we were all wet, and Corinne was absolutely filthy, so could we borrow some clothes?

'Sure won't ye just get wet again the minute ye go back out?' she asked distractedly as she tried to absorb all that information.

'True. Oh well, we'll get a taxi then,' I said. Just as well I still had twenty quid in my wallet.

'So what was all that about, then? The last time she came over?' Danielle whispered.

'If I only knew!' I whispered back. 'All I know is that she never went out with Rob, if that's any use to you.'

'Do you know, I don't think I even care anymore,' she told me. 'The whole thing gets worse by the day, and I can't take much more of it.'

'Don't worry about it,' I said. 'Because worrying hasn't got me anywhere.'

Just then a heavier than usual gust of wind banged the door against the wall and a storm wave of wind poured into the hall.

'God Almighty!' said Danielle, shutting the door behind Corinne, who was still hovering around the doorstep. 'Come on up and I'll see what I've got.'

Corinne followed us upstairs. Thankfully, Danielle's flatmate, who I'd never met, had gone home for the weekend, so she was on her own. She put on the kettle in the kitchen and I took off my jacket and boots, which were soaked right through. Then I looked at Corinne in the light of the bare bulb, and I realized just how awful she appeared, with her clothes and hands caked in mud and dead leaves and with make-up streaked all down her face.

'Jesus, Corinne, you'd better have a wash,' I said. 'Can she have a shower, Danielle?' I called into the kitchen.

'Yeah, whatever,' she answered, coming into the room. 'I'll

just show you where the bathroom is and get you some towels,' she told Corinne without looking at her.

Danielle obviously didn't know what to make of the situation, but even still, she showed Corinne where everything was and lent her jeans and a top. They were way too big for Corinne, but it was better than being too small.

'Thanks a million, Danielle. I really appreciate this,' I said when Corinne had gone into the bathroom. I was feeling guilty now for having been so pissed off the time Hannah made me spend that Friday night here with her.

'No problem,' she said. 'Are your clothes as wet as hers?'

'No, I think it's just my socks and trousers,' I said.

'I can lend you some of mine.'

I got changed in her room. Her clothes were closer to my size than Corinne's, so her jeans were only a bit loose on me. When I was ready, I went back into the sitting room and spread out the wet jackets on a chair beside the heater. Danielle came out of the kitchen with two cups of tea and sat down on the couch beside me. Then she whispered, 'So, have you any idea at all what's going on?' I really did not know what to say to her or where to begin. But Rob walked in then, as wet and filthy as Corinne. Danielle immediately stiffened and stared intently at the blank television screen.

'Here,' he said, handing me a plastic bag with two sets of burger and chips in it.

'Thanks,' I said.

He stood uneasily in the middle of the room, looking at the floor. Then he said to Danielle, 'I didn't get you anything because I'd no money.'

She ignored him and went into the kitchen. There was an awkward silence for a minute. Then I told him that Corinne was in the shower and that maybe he should have one himself. When he had disappeared, I called Danielle back into the room.

'It's bad, isn't it?' she said. 'Whatever's going on, it must be pretty bad.' She looked upset, and I didn't know what to say to her.

'Here, have some of my chips,' I said finally, unwrapping all the paper around them.

'No thanks, I'm not hungry.'

Corinne wandered in at that stage, looking a bit better than she had been, in spite of the fact that she was swamped inside Danielle's clothes, which were incredibly loose and baggy on her. But she was clean, and she had even combed her wet hair out. Nevertheless, she was very restless and fidgety, and she only ate about two chips and a mouthful of burger, saying that she'd get sick if she ate any more. She sat on the couch beside me, staring into space and pulling at the torn patch on its arm while Danielle threw her intense, searching looks. It got very awkward, and I was getting anxious about what would happen over at Mr Johnson's, so I pushed away my own uneaten chips and said that it was getting late, that we'd better head off. Even though it was only about half-seven. Still though, I could see through the window that it was dark now.

'I'll ring you a taxi,' said Danielle, and she disappeared downstairs.

I threw Corinne her boots and put my own on. They were still wet of course, but because they were warm from the heater, they didn't feel quite so bad on as they should.

'It'll be here in ten minutes,' said Danielle. 'So do you want to leave your wet stuff here or take it with you?'

'Oh, I'll take it out of your way,' I said.

She gave me a few plastic bags, and I stuffed everything into them.

'Listen, Danielle, thanks a million for everything,' I said. 'And I'll get your stuff back to you as soon as possible, OK?'

'Oh yeah, whatever. Well, good luck,' she told me, standing at the door of her flat. Then she looked hesitantly at Corinne and said goodbye to her.

Me and Corinne called for Rob. He'd had his shower and he'd changed into another pair of old jeans that were clean. Silently, we went down to the hall and waited for the taxi. Five more minutes and we were on our way.

Twenty-four

It was nearly eight o'clock when we got to Mr Johnson's. The house stood tall and hostile against the storm. Not the slightest chink of light escaped from the windows. Rob and Corinne followed me reluctantly up the steep steps and stood behind me while I knocked on the door. Twice. Waited with a high-pitched, heart-exploding anxiety. There was no answer and I blamed the low, dull door knocker. The presence of Rob and Corinne hung heavily behind me, radiating waves of tension. Oh God, please let them be in. I knocked one more time, as loudly as I could. This time I heard footsteps, and a few seconds later, the door opened. Mr Johnson stood there. At first he looked surprised. Then his face went into neutral.

'Merle, this is a surprise,' he said, studying Corinne. 'And would this be your sister?'

'It is, yeah,' I said. 'And this is Rob.'

'I thought as much,' he said, eyeing Rob critically from head to toe. I was glad now that all the muck and stuff were gone off them. 'Well, come in out of the rain,' he said, stepping out of the doorway.

We followed him into the sitting room where Shane was sitting on the couch beside the dying fire.

'How's it going, Shane?' I asked, talking fast and saying

anything and everything because I was so nervous. 'It's a rotten night, isn't it? God, this place is like a furnace.'

'Yes, it's nice and warm now,' said Mr Johnson, sitting down beside Shane and taking up about three-quarters of the couch. 'We had the fire lit earlier, but the wind kept blowing the smoke back down the chimney, so we had to abandon it and put the heating on instead. Sit down, please.'

Corinne and Rob sat on the couch opposite the fireplace, as far away as they could from Shane and Mr Johnson. I was going to sit there with them, but something made me stay clear of them and I sat instead on the chair facing Shane and Mr Johnson, clutching my jacket and the two bags filled with wet clothes.

'Shane, take their coats and put them outside,' said Mr Johnson. 'And why don't you bring up some tea or coffee? Which would you prefer?' he asked us.

'Tea, please,' I said.

He looked inquiringly at Corinne and Rob, but they didn't answer.

'Actually, we'll all have tea,' I said quickly to cover their silence. 'So, did you have a good weekend?' I asked Mr Johnson.

I almost didn't know what I was saying to him, I was too busy worrying about what was going to happen when he started asking questions about what we were doing here. Because as soon as I tell him, he'll dismiss it all out of hand and that'll be the end of it. Corinne can do what she wants then. Oh God.

But Mr Johnson didn't ask me what the story was. I could swear that he knew by looking at us that there was trouble of some kind brewing. And he seemed determined to keep a lid on it by spinning out a steady stream of chitchat about the weather, and about how he was so glad he'd gotten double-glazing on the windows – it really kept out the draughts – and about how good it had been to see Hannah on Friday night, and so on.

Shane came back in with a tray, which he left on a table in the middle of the room before sitting down again. After looking at him closely, Mr Johnson got up and poured the tea, handing us each a cup. Corinne and Rob just looked at him, and as soon as they'd taken their cups into their hands, they put them down on the floor without having drunk a mouthful.

'Well, it's good to meet you two after hearing so much about you,' Mr Johnson said to Corinne and Rob, looking at their cups. Again, they didn't answer.

'Yeah, they were just saying tonight how nice it'd be to see Shane again,' I babbled, realizing even as I said it how stupid it sounded.

'Really?' said Mr Johnson ironically. 'Well, that's good to hear, isn't it, Shane?'

Corinne and Rob followed his eyes as they turned to rest on Shane, who remained sullen and silent. I got the impression that Mr Johnson was getting a bit worried about Shane, who was unnervingly still, and, looking at his watch, Mr Johnson exclaimed that he had no idea it was so late, and that there were a few things he had to do tonight.

'Let me get you your coats,' he said, standing up.

'We don't want them,' I said quickly.

'Oh?' he asked coolly.

'Well, what I meant to say was, you know, that they're wet, so they wouldn't be much use to us.'

'But it's better to have them than not to have them,' he said firmly and left the room.

This is crazy, I told myself while we were waiting for him to come back into the room. You can't let him make you leave before doing what you came here for.

'Just one more thing before we go,' I said nervously when he'd returned. 'I was hoping Shane could tell me what the connection is between the three of them.'

'We've had this conversation before,' said Mr Johnson angrily.

'Let's not get into it again!' and he practically threw the jackets at me.

Corinne's hand seemed to shake as she took her jacket off me, but she put it on quickly, and she and Rob practically ran out of the room and into the hall. Mr Johnson told Shane that he was going to see us out, but when Shane didn't answer, he frowned and sat down beside him, telling me to see ourselves out. I went into the hall, closing the door behind me. Corinne was trying to open the front door, but her hand was shaking and she couldn't manage it.

'Slow down, Corinne,' I told her. 'We can't let your man send us packing until we've talked to Shane. That was the deal, remember?'

'Wild horses wouldn't drag me back in there again,' she said, moving aside to let Rob have a go at the door.

'Yeah, Merle. Leave her alone,' said Rob, twisting the key and cursing when he discovered that he'd just double-locked the door.

'Why? What's the problem?' I asked, more certain than ever that there was something up.

'Nothing, it's just, I want to go home now,' said Corinne.

'Why? Because you're screwed up about Rob and Shane?' I persisted. 'OK, look, it's up to you. You can go home if you want, but first of all, you have to come back in there with me for five minutes while I talk to Shane.'

Rob had now succeeded in getting the door open, and looked at Corinne as if to say come on, let's get out of here, but she hesitated.

'OK,' she told me.

Reluctantly, Rob closed the door and followed us. I opened the sitting room door, and we three saw Mr Johnson sitting on the couch with his arm around Shane, speaking words I can't remember because at that point, Corinne screamed.

'I thought you'd left!' said Mr Johnson furiously. 'Would you like to tell me what the hell is going on here?'

Corinne had grabbed Rob's arm and was shaking so much that he had to bring her back to the couch where they both sat down again. Stunned by the sound of that scream, I closed the door and sat down again on my chair.

'Are you OK?' I asked Corinne.

'I feel like I've walked in on a nightmare and discovered that it's actually real,' she said.

'What's she talking about?' asked Mr Johnson.

'Ask Shane,' I answered, my eyes on Corinne.

'Well, Shane?' asked Mr Johnson, but Shane cowered at the sound of his voice and seated himself as far as he could into the corner of their couch so that he wasn't touching up against him.

'OK, Little Miss Clever,' said Mr Johnson to me furiously, springing to his feet. 'I think it's about time we had a little talk, don't you?'

'What do you mean?' I asked, standing up so as to be less intimidated by his height.

'You know very well what I mean. Just what do you intend to achieve by barging in here and upsetting Shane like this?'

'I just wanted to talk to him about something.'

'Just wanted to talk to him? You obviously have some kind of game plan in mind, and I want to know what it is, you little . . .' He broke off and shook me by the shoulders.

Just then, Corinne cried out, 'Don't do it to her! You can't!'

Mr Johnson stopped in his tracks. 'Do what to her?'

Something disruptive and terrible seemed to have gone off inside Corinne, and it was intensified by the sound of his voice.

'Oh my God, it's true, isn't it Rob?' she said. She grabbed his arm so tight it looked excruciatingly painful.

'What's true?' I asked her.

She looked up at me slowly. 'I don't know,' she said. 'Ever

since I first saw Shane a month ago, I feel like I'm living in a dream, only I can't see what it is, because it's surrounded by clouds and shadows, and every time they lift, I see or feel something horrible, so I pull them back down again. And then just now, I realize that everything in that dream is real, that the room is real, the candles are real, and, and Beauty and the Beast is real. Oh God, why did I have to remember.'

Rob stared at her in disbelief. 'How could you ever forget?' It was the first time he'd spoken since entering the room and his voice was strange: hoarse as if he'd been shouting all night, but also unsure and unused, as if he'd never spoken a word in his life. 'Did you forget, Shane?' he asked. It was like he could hardly bring himself to look at Shane, managed it only after a huge struggle. Shane looked away. But Rob went over to him. 'Did you, Shane?' he asked. Shane didn't answer. Rob turned to Corinne. 'But you must have remembered,' he said. 'Why else did you come to see me then, twice, after all these years of not talking?'

'I don't know. I don't even remember having ever been friendly with you. In fact, I always hated you without knowing why. But then, when I was carrying this nightmare around with me, I suddenly got this feeling that you were the only one who would understand about it without me having to say a word. It only makes sense to me now, seeing him again.' She pointed to Mr Johnson and shuddered.

'So you did see him in the pub with Shane,' I said.

'Yeah.'

'But what did he do to you that was so bad you forgot it till now?' I asked.

'What I did? This is ridiculous! I'm not listening to any more of this,' said Mr Johnson.

Corinne flinched at his voice. 'He didn't do anything.' Her

voice broke down and then she whispered, 'He just reminded me of someone.'

'Does he remind you of anyone, Shane?' Rob asked, his voice all choked up.

Shane didn't answer.

'Will someone please tell me what this is all about?' Again, Mr Johnson's voice had a repelling effect on the other three. He saw this and, bewildered and out of his depth, he sat on the chair facing Rob and Corinne.

'Say it, Rob,' said Corinne slowly. 'So I'll know if it's true or not. Because even though I know it's real, it's now such a magnified real that it can't be true, can it?'

'Oh, it's true alright,' said Rob harshly, and a short silence fell.

'Please, Rob,' I begged him. 'You have to tell her.'

'Jesus Christ,' he said. He paused for a moment and then he continued reluctantly. 'When we were all six, our mams made us go to drama classes in the Community Centre. There were piles of kids there, but me, Corinne and Shane got picked out to . . . to star in this play, *Beauty and the Beast*. She was Beauty, I was her da, and Shane was the Beast.' It was getting so difficult for him to talk that he had to stop here.

'We were meant to have it ready for Christmas, and Teacher was worried about the way it was shaping up, so he said the three of us would have to have some extra classes. "Oh yeah, whatever," our mams said. They were so excited about it, and I suppose we were too. I know I was so proud to have been picked out, though I was a bit afraid of making mistakes, because that made Teacher angry, and I didn't like that. Anyway, one night . . .'

Rob got up off the couch, agitated and troubled, and went over to the fireplace, where he seemed to lose himself, staring into the dying embers. I lit a smoke, wanting to still my own shaking hands, and I offered him one, but he didn't take it. Leaning against the fireplace, his eyes still fixed on the expiring coals, he pulled himself together again and resumed his story.

'Maybe it wasn't night, because it was the winter, but it was pitch dark, anyway. Teacher brought us into the hall, and locked the door behind him, saying he didn't want anyone to disturb us. He left the key in the lock, and I can still see it there, that and the other keys on the ring, glaring at me, warning me that I'd better be good tonight. He said we were going to run through it just like it would be on the day, so he didn't put on the lights in the hall, just a few of the lights on the stage. Then he lit a few candles, and put them on the table. And he gave me a cloak to wear, and Corinne got a pile of necklaces. She said she didn't like them, that they were too tight around her neck, but he told her he went to great trouble to get them, so she kept quiet about it after that, though she kept pulling and pulling at them, trying to loosen them up. And Shane . . . Shane was the Beast, so he got one of them Halloween masks. And he kept mouthing off too, about how it was sweaty and it scratched his face and could he take it off. Teacher got angry then, you could see it in the way he looked at us. He sat down on the big chair that was kind of like a throne and he said quietly that he hadn't realized what ungrateful brats we were, that he thought we were good children, that he thought we . . . liked him. And Shane . . . Shane said we were sorry, that we'd be good. And then he pulled Shane up on his knee . . . And then . . .'

Rob turned to me. 'Do I really have to say this? Can't you just . . . guess the rest?'

I looked over at Corinne. She was staring at the floor with unfocused eyes that struggled between the need to express what she was hearing and the need to push it away. But she couldn't push it away again, or else this cycle of tortured dreams and self-destruction would just go on and on. As for Shane, his face was buried into the couch where I couldn't see it, while Mr Johnson looked both disturbed and anxious to hear what came next.

'Please, Rob.' I said. 'I really do need to know what happened.'

'OK, then,' he said finally, with a huge effort. 'Basically, what happened was . . . Teacher was doing Shane on the big chair, and me and Corinne were standing there, scared out of our wits, Corinne pulling at the necklaces around her neck. And I, I just couldn't take it. So I told Teacher to stop, and he shouted at me to go away, and I was absolutely terrified. And then it was Corinne's turn . . . She was crying for us to help her, please, so I told Teacher again, and he said to be quiet, that I'd be next. So when he came to grab me, I ran all over the stage, but then he caught me and pinned me down on the big chair. Teacher was doing me, and I was lashing out, trying to get away. I grabbed the table-cloth on the nearby table and pulled it. The candles fell over, starting a little fire. I was still pinned underneath him, and he was trying to put the fire out with one hand. I wriggled free and caught the leg of the table. He lurched after me, so I swung around the table, and the force of his movement and the swing of the table unbalanced him and he fell off the stage and crashed his head on the ground below. We looked over, and we saw him dazed, trying to get up. He rose to his knees, fixing his trousers and tucking his shirt back in. Then he looked up at us, and I'll never forget the look he gave us – his head was bleeding, and there was blood dripping down his face. Then he collapsed, so we, we thought he was dead. The fire was taking hold, so the three of us ran to the door, unlocked it, and then ran outside as fast as we could, shouting for help.'

The unlocked secret of the darkness smashed the room with its implications.

'Oh my God,' I said softly.

Corinne was crying now. I went over to her and took her on to my shoulder.

'Did you really forget about it, until tonight?' Rob asked her with a tremor in his voice.

'I don't know,' she said, 'I, I didn't remember it, but even still, I think it was always there, somewhere in the depths of my mind.'

And what about Shane, I wondered. But his face was still hidden, and I was too shocked to speak to him.

'So what happened next?' I urged Rob.

'Oh,' he said. 'There were about three or four people out on the road, and they came running as fast as they could. And then the commotion attracted piles more. God, I'll never forget it. One minute, the building was quiet and deserted, and the next, it was swarming with people shouting "Fire!". Someone pulled Teacher out while someone else rang for an ambulance and a fire brigade. And Teacher was still conscious, so he told them it was all an accident, that he knocked over the table and fell off the stage. The three of us just stood there in the middle of it, lost and confused, while everyone around us seemed to be running and shouting and banging into us. All these different voices, going on about what a terrible accident it was. Nobody passed any heed of us.'

'I can imagine,' I said, picturing the scene to myself. 'So what happened to the teacher?'

'He died that night in hospital.' Rob dropped his voice even lower. 'He'd fractured his skull.'

There was a silence for a few minutes while everyone tried to absorb that.

'And did you ever tell anyone what really happened?' I asked, trying to make sense of the whole thing.

'What do you think?' he asked roughly.

'Of course not,' I said. 'Stupid question, really.'

'That kind of guilt really fucks up your head,' said Rob. 'But as for Shane . . .' He turned to Shane, who looked up at him and then away again. Rob continued, 'I just don't understand you,

212

Shane. When I saw you with your boyfriend in town one day, the whole thing came back to life. It was like, how could you pick someone so like that teacher and, and live with him?'

Shane didn't answer. Mr Johnson jumped up, all indignation. He marched over to the couch where Shane was sitting, and snarled at Rob that that was going too far, but Rob ignored him.

'I mean, how could you, Shane?' continued Rob. 'I followed you home, you know. I stood across the road for hours, staring at your window, wondering if, if when you were with your boyfriend, you remembered what *he* had done, all those years ago.'

'That's outrageous! Absolutely outrageous!' exclaimed Mr Johnson. He sat down beside Shane and put his hand on his shoulder. 'You don't have to listen to this, Shane.'

Shane tore away from him and stood up, backing away. 'Don't come near me,' he said.

'Don't do this Shane,' said Mr Johnson rising, genuinely disturbed, but anxious to re-establish his authority. 'I knew nothing about any of this, ever,' he said firmly. 'It wasn't like that, was it? I know you had your dark moments, when you withdrew from me completely, but I put that down to getting over the drugs.'

'I don't know what it was like,' said Shane in a heightened, tense voice. 'Just leave me alone, will you?'

'Come on Shane,' persisted Mr Johnson.

'I said leave me alone!' Shane shouted angrily, turning his face in towards the fireplace so that he didn't have to look at him.

Mr Johnson turned on us. 'You'd better leave now!' he ordered.

'Don't worry, I'm going,' said Rob. 'Come with us Shane. Don't let him make you stay here.'

Shane remained frozen. I saw his face partially reflected in the blurred, grey mirror, and it had been distorted into dark shapelessness. Mr Johnson opened the door and stood there, waiting for us to leave. I thought it was better to go, because I was afraid of what further effect his hostility might have on Corinne, but for a moment, I resisted being thrown out of the room.

'What do you want me to tell Hannah?' I asked Shane, hoping that might get through to him.

He kept his back to us, but I could see he was shaking. Mr Johnson was taking no chances of losing him. He bundled us out into the dark hall, closing the sitting room door behind him. He flung the front door open, and stood silently, watching us walk down the steps. As we reached the gate, I heard Shane call my name. I turned around, and saw him standing there, shaking.

'Tell Hannah I'm sorry,' he said.

I looked up at him through the cold, life-affirming rain, and searched for a word that I could say to reach him. But all I could manage was 'I will,' before the door was closed on him, swallowing him up in its own eternal darkness.

Twenty-five

It was about ten when we left that house. We wandered, dazed and drenched, back towards the bright, living main street that teemed with rain. We paused there, unable to bring ourselves to even speak and make a decision about what to do next, watching the people running past us into the warm, dry shop or the chipper or the Chinese take-away. In our state of mind, they were all like aliens from a strange, comfortable, protected world. Eventually, I said we'd better go home – it seemed the only thing to do. I couldn't think of anywhere else to go, and none of us were in a state for talking, anyway. That stirred Corinne a bit and she said, 'Do we have to go home? I don't want to talk to Mam tonight, I'm too tired.'

'Well, we can't just hang around here all night,' I said. 'And I can't think of anywhere to go. But don't worry about it. Just say you're tired and you're going straight to bed.'

Corinne obviously wasn't ready to talk about it yet – not to Mam anyway, which was understandable. I couldn't believe that could have happened without anyone copping on. Still though, in those days, people didn't suspect such things. And besides, there must have been so much drama and commotion that night that if people noticed something wrong with the kids they would have put it down to the shock of their teacher knocking the table over and falling off the stage, setting the whole place on fire.

They'd never in a million years have thought he fell in a tussle with a six-year-old boy.

'Does, does this mean you're not going to try to kill yourself again?' I asked Corinne, incapable of holding that back any longer.

'I don't know,' she said slowly. 'I don't know. What are you going to do, Rob?'

He shrank back from the question. 'Would you two mind if I just went off now?' he asked uncomfortably. 'You don't have to worry about me, I'm not going to do anything. But I need to walk around for a bit, think things through, you know?'

We watched him disappear, a small dark shadow on the orange-hued, water-blurred lights of the night-town. I tried to light a smoke in the face of the storm, but the wind was so strong that I had to give up.

'I hope he'll be alright,' I said.

'I don't know,' said Corinne. 'I think it might be worse this way. I wonder if, when I wake up tomorrow, the relief I feel now'll be gone, and only the pain'll be left. How am I going to live with that?'

'You'll be alright,' I said, not knowing whether she would be or not, but wanting to reassure her as much as possible. 'At least now, you'll have something to fight, something you can focus on.'

The buses brought us home to the temporary oblivion of sleep. Corinne went into her own room, where the burnt curtains and the smell had gone. And I sat up most of the night in a state of shock, reliving the past night in pure horror-stricken disbelief.

The rain was gone the following morning, but the dark clouds continued to hang low, almost scratching the rooftops. Corinne was still asleep when I heard the doorbell ring around nine. I opened the door anxiously, wondering what repercussions the night might have brought on. It was Hannah, looking shocked, as if she knew something.

'Shane's dead,' she said.

Minutes passed as I stood there in a stunned silence.

'I thought I'd better tell you,' she said. 'Seeing as you won't know from the news.'

'Oh?' I asked.

'Yeah. They'll just say a car crash. They can't name them until Mr Johnson's next of kin's been informed, and that's going to take a while to figure out.'

'Oh,' I said.

Then Hannah asked me could we go somewhere to talk about it, some place where we wouldn't see anyone or be reminded of anything. I reckoned Corinne was safe enough for the time being, so I silently followed Hannah outside.

Where can you go that's free of associations without at least getting on a bus? We ended up walking a long way out on to the main road before sitting down on the side like hitchhikers in the summer. It was cold, but worth it.

She talked and chain-smoked. I listened. But even though Hannah spoke to me, she barely seemed to know I was there. It was as if she was trying to make sense of everything to herself rather than explaining it to someone else.

'There was a car crash late last night,' said Hannah. 'Shane was driving and Mr Johnson was in the car with him. They'd been drinking in this yuppie pub that's on a main road and they didn't leave until the last minute, when the place was closing up. Then they went outside, got into the car, and Shane set off at high speed. They ran into a concrete wall. The car caught fire. Both of them died. Someone told Mam earlier this morning and she woke me up, but she didn't know what to say really. I told her I'd been to see them and stuff. If I hadn't met them, it mightn't have been so bad, but I had. Oh God.'

And that's my fault. Hannah wouldn't have been anywhere near them if it hadn't been for me dragging her over there in the first place. But for me, this chain of events wouldn't have even started. What have I done?

'Was your mam angry with you?' I asked.

'Oh, I don't know. She was shouting at me alright, but I don't know what that meant.'

I smoked in silence, worried at what I'd have to tell Hannah, to illuminate for her the horror and the logic of what Shane had done.

'What do the guards think happened?' I asked.

'Oh, there has to be an investigation, and they're doing a post-mortem on the bodies at the moment.'

'Yeah, but have they no idea at all?' I persisted.

'Well, loads of people were drinking in the pub, and they'd left around the same time, so they'd seen Shane and Mr Johnson getting into the car and Shane driving off . . . So the guards reckon it was a drink-driving accident.'

It looked like no one would suspect Shane of having crashed the car deliberately. Thank God. Some things were better left unsaid.

'Did the people in the pub say what kind of form him and Mr Johnson were in?' I asked, wondering if they'd been fighting.

'I don't know. I didn't ask any of that. One thing at a time, Merle. I'm still trying to let it all sink in.'

But Hannah had a right to know what had happened last night. So I told her that once there was a fairy-tale, *Beauty and the Beast,* and some sick bastard of a drama teacher projected all his fantasies on to it. So he chose three beautiful children, Shane for the Beast, Rob for the da, and Corinne for Beauty, and turned the fairy-tale into a horror story. Just one night was enough to kill their lives, leaving nothing but ghosts behind. The darkness laid Rob to waste, burying him under a smoky cloud that prevented him from ever doing anything constructive with his life. Corinne was like a haunted shell, possessed by the weight of suppressed memory, and driven to complete the cycle of destruction by trying to kill herself. And Shane turned to drugs, seeking to escape into the oblivion offered by heroin.

But Shane had the bad luck to be trapped for the second time, by Mr Johnson, who reminded Rob, Corinne and surely Shane of that drama teacher. Shane must have tried to suppress that resemblance. Or maybe Mr Johnson didn't look at all like that teacher – maybe he reminded the other two of him only because they saw him with Shane. Either way, last night, Corinne finally remembered and Rob and Shane admitted what had happened when they were six. It must have been too much for Shane to bear. Shane was fucked up, he couldn't have cared about Mr Johnson. But Mr Johnson was the sort of person who insisted on getting his own way, so Shane must have just let him take him over completely. And then last night, Shane must have decided to end that control, in the only way he knew how.

'He said to tell you he was sorry,' I told Hannah.

'Sorry,' she said bloodlessly, 'sorry for what in particular?'

'Everything, I suppose. For scaring the shit out of you as a kid, for not being there for you now, and for killing himself.'

Hannah fiddled with the lighter in silence and then lit up again. 'Oh, he had nothing to be sorry about,' she said bitterly. 'It was all out of his control. I mean, even Corinne tried to top herself, didn't she? But I can't help thinking, why did it have to be like that? Corinne and Rob aren't dead, are they?'

'It was different for Shane. He had no other way out. But I don't know about the other two . . . Jesus, do you think they're alright? Look, would you be able to go to my house and stay with Corinne till I get back? She's probably still asleep, but if she isn't, I know she wouldn't mind you knowing, so tell her I told you everything and explain to her about Shane. Rob's the one I'd be most worried about, so I'd better go over there now.'

'Why him?' Hannah asked as we walked back towards the houses.

I stopped at a bus stop. 'Because he has no one, whereas I don't think Corinne would do anything without telling me first.' She flinched, so I added, 'Mr Johnson had a stronger hold on Shane than you did. What happened wasn't your fault, Hannah.'

And then she left for Corinne, walking down the grey road while I waited impatiently for a bus.

Twenty-six

My anxiety grew as I walked down the road towards Rob's. The ground was cold with the bitterness of the approaching winter, and the cold spread upwards, as if it was reaching up to bite the clouds. I rang Rob's bell twice, but there was no answer. And I was still in such a daze from last night and this morning that it took me several minutes to realize the front door was open. I went upstairs to find Rob lying on his couch, staring up at the cracked ceiling. The silence was total, so he must have heard the bell. I thought about leaving, but decided it was better to say what I'd come here for.

'Shane's dead,' I said.

He didn't say anything, didn't even move. I shook the dust from a cushion on the floor and sat on it. Then I took the last smoke out of my box, vaguely registering that I'd now smoked a whole box since nine o clock this morning. Eventually, Rob sat up and asked me to tell him about Shane. Riven by pain, he blamed himself, saying that he shouldn't have attacked Shane about Mr Johnson. I told him it wasn't his fault, that Shane would have had to admit the reality of the relationship to himself at some stage. And if he hadn't? I reckoned Shane was better off where he was now, that he had some kind of freedom, no matter how dark.

'What about you?' I asked, my mind replaying all Rob had said last night to illuminate that strange bond between him and Corinne and Shane. He didn't answer me, just looked around the bare, decaying room, as I said, 'What did you do last night, after you left us?'

'Oh, not much, just, you know, walked and walked around the place for hours.'

Like he used to do after he had first seen Shane and Mr Johnson together – walk for hours, stand staring at their windows and then walk some more. The light was duller and greyer than I ever remembered it being in this room before, and I felt as if all the glamour, all the promises of excitement and fulfilment that had ever steeped themselves into the walls, glistening but unattainable, had never been more than some stupid, childish fantasy of mine. Me who had never known how all the early promise of what Rob might have been had been stunted and shattered. He had been reduced to the unthreatening misery of this isolated room with its broken mirror and a few threadbare silk scarves – I had thought they were supposed to be atmospheric, but now I understood that this room was a shadow re-creation, a self-destructive reference to another room, another stage.

'Have you told Danielle about any of this?' I asked him.

Rob took a tape out of his pocket and gave it to me. It was an ordinary cassette with nothing written on it, but one that had been handled a lot.

'What's on it?' I asked.

It was the sort of cassette you buy to tape other people's CDs or to tape bits of your own music so that you can listen to what your playing sounds like. Rob was nervous and unsure, last night having obviously used up most of his strength.

'I found it with a note under the door last night when I got back,' he said. 'It's her.'

I turned it over in my hands and thought of him coming back

here broken and alone in the rain last night, and then sitting for hours, listening to it over and over again. If I was to press play, then I would hear Danielle's voice lacerating Rob. Only how was she to know that it wasn't his fault, that an iron fist had long ago crushed any chance of their having a relationship. Oh God. I'm hurting, but it's not sympathy that's hurting me. To feel sorry for them would mean feeling separate from all this, and I don't. Right now I share the hurt of all these people.

'I don't want to hear this,' I said. 'I don't think I should.' He didn't say anything, but the heavy silence hit me and I said, 'But I'll listen to it if you want me to.'

'It doesn't matter,' he said. 'I just wanted to sort things out before I went.'

'Why don't you tell me what she says instead?'

Because that would probably seem harder, having to relate it himself instead of hiding behind the tape. But for me it would be harder hearing her voice in front of him, after all that had happened last night.

'Danielle just says the usual,' said Rob, breaking the silence. 'You know, I'm a bastard, and she never wants to see me again, all that kind of stuff. Then she says she's moving out of the house today so that she doesn't have to worry about running into me.'

'Are you sorry?'

'In some ways I am, in some ways I amn't. It's probably better alright, but it's a pity it had to be like this.'

And a pity it had to end like this, with no explanations. Danielle would never know why he had treated her so badly. Would never understand that he had cared about her, but that he had been so fucked up by the events of one night that he was incapable of treating her any other way. One black-starred night that had been resurrected the minute he first saw Shane with Mr Johnson.

'And to think she thought you were going out with Corinne,' I said ironically.

He didn't answer. We sat there awhile, each of us with our own thoughts. I wondered how I was going to get Danielle's clothes back to her now, but that question soon faded as the events of yesterday and today crept back up on me.

'Well, I'd better be getting back to Corinne,' I said finally. 'Are you sure you want to be on your own? Because if you want, you can come home with me.'

'No, I'll be alright,' he said. 'But thanks for asking.'

And so I left him there.

Twenty-seven

I felt a bit calmer as I walked away from Rob's. The sky remained as overcast as ever, but the daylight brightened for a moment, making the last pools of yesterday's rain shine.

I got the bus and headed for home, remembering to buy more cigarettes on the way. Maybe it had been thoughtless to leave Hannah so long with Corinne, but things had worked out when I got back. Hannah had told Mam about Shane's death, so she thought Hannah had come over to our house looking for sympathy and sanctuary from her own home until the atmosphere over there had lightened. I don't think Hannah and Corinne had talked about it much, if at all. After the initial explanations, they had sat in silence, too preoccupied with the enormity of it all to do anything else.

Me and Hannah promised to help Corinne get over it, as soon as our minds began to function again. Meanwhile, we waited. Paid our last respects to Shane, who was given a family funeral that seemed so unreal and so out of place to me that I had to convince myself it was really happening. I thought it was all a strange trick of the light and that, if I reached out and touched it, it would disintegrate.

Rob came to the funeral and spent a long, mostly silent, night in the pub with me, Corinne and Hannah. We all sat at a table where pain cut so deep into us that we drank as much as we could in an effort to blunt its edge. Hannah told us that the post-mortem had shown excessive levels of alcohol in the blood-streams of both bodies, so the guards had presumed it was a drink-driving accident alright. There would be an inquest in about three months time, but the finding would almost certainly be death by misadventure. When I asked Hannah, she said that the barman in the pub had said that Shane and Mr Johnson had seemed to be having a bit of an argument alright, but nobody had passed any heed of it. The two names never even made the news or the paper, because by the time it was OK to release Mr Johnson's name to the public, the crash was no longer a news item. There were too many drink-driving accidents for anyone to bat an eyelid.

Thank God, I thought. But afterwards, I was haunted by images of what must have happened that night after we left. Shane and Mr Johnson must have argued and argued. And then maybe Shane said that he couldn't stand staying in that room any longer, not after what had been said there, that he wanted to go out, anywhere at all, he didn't care where. 'Don't be ridiculous,' says Mr Johnson in my imagination. 'There's a storm outside.' But he and Shane drive up to this pub anyway. I think Mr Johnson chooses it, because it's a pub that's popular with an older, yuppie crowd, more his territory than Shane's, and he desperately needs to reassert himself after what's happened. So obviously the arguing is a lot less heated in the pub, but things are far from settled. They won't be settled until they sit in that car and Shane turns the key in the ignition.

An old friend of Mr Johnson's from America had his body brought back out there. When Mr Johnson's previous boyfriend had died from cancer, he had said that he wanted to be buried with him. This friend had known about Shane, and told Hannah that the crash was a terrible tragedy, that Mr Johnson had been so happy with him.

Twenty-eight

Corinne was quiet for the next few days. She said that she was still letting it all sink in. She kept pretty much to herself, though she'd come out with me for a walk in the afternoons if I wasn't working. And she came out with me and Hannah on Saturday night. Hannah was also pretty quiet and preoccupied that night, her thoughts full of Shane and all I had told her of the dreadful night of the crash. But she mentioned that she had run into Danielle in college. Danielle had given Hannah her new phone number and had asked her to get the clothes back off me.

'Yeah, I'll drop them in to you tomorrow,' I told Hannah.

'That'd be great,' she said. 'But as well as that, Danielle wanted to know what happened that night after you left her.'

'What did you say?' Corinne asked nervously.

'I just said that the three of you went and confronted my brother about something, but I didn't know what it was. "Oh yeah, Shane's my brother, in case you didn't know," I said. And then I told her that I really did not want to talk about it, seeing as Shane went out afterwards and got completely scuttered and ended up getting himself killed in a car crash.'

'That was probably the best thing to say alright,' I said. 'So she hasn't been talking to Rob at all, then?'

'No, and she's not going to be either,' said Hannah. 'As far as she's concerned, she's well rid of him.'

'Oh well,' I said, wondering how Rob was – he'd said he'd ring and he hadn't. I decided to go and see him tomorrow and ask him if there was anything he wanted to say to Danielle.

The next day was raw, but clear. As I walked up the stairs to Rob's flat, I noticed that the place seemed very quiet and empty. As I opened his unlocked door, I got the impression that his flat was still and bare. I looked closer and saw that this was because the room was clean and all his stuff was cleared out. Wondering anxiously if he was gone for good, I looked outside at the shadowed sunlight and the overgrown wilderness of the garden and saw smoke rising ominously from behind a decrepit shed at the bottom of the garden. Corinne had tried to destroy the room in her memory by setting her curtains on fire. Shane died by fire. And Rob . . .

The backdoor was stiff and jammed. I pulled violently at it to open and eventually I succeeded. The grass was so high and tangled that it was easy to pick out and follow the path Rob had trodden. He was standing in front of a bonfire, watching it with the stillness of a corpse.

'What are you burning?' I asked him.

He hadn't seen me coming, but even still, he didn't react to my appearance or presence. He didn't even look at me.

'Everything I can't sell,' he said quietly.

'Because you want to get rid of the past?' I asked, relieved that he wasn't getting rid of himself.

'Because I don't want to have to carry it around with me any-more.'

We stood awhile in the sharp glare of the relentlessly consuming flames. Eventually, Rob put the fire out.

'No one else'll come out here because of the rats,' he said. 'I wonder if I made the problem better or worse? It doesn't affect me, anyway. I'm not staying here another night.'

We went back inside, sat on the floor in the cold flat. Where'll you go?' I asked him. America, he said, to work for an uncle who had a garage there. He should have gone years ago, he said, stupid of him not to have really, but he couldn't. And now, he had to, there was no other way for him to go.

'What about Danielle?' I asked him. 'Hannah's back in touch with her, you know, if, if you want to say goodbye.'

'No, it's OK,' he said. 'I wouldn't know what to say to her.'

'Are you sure?' I persisted. 'It seems a pity to leave unfinished business behind you.'

'No, it's for the best,' he said. 'Anyway, it's time to move on.'

Time to leave. Leave, I thought, that's what me and Corinne should do too. Leave the landscape of suppression and darkness behind us.

'Where's your guitar?' I asked, wanting to initiate a normal conversation, so that I could remember that, just once, we'd had one. I want all that's happened to mean that we can at least communicate properly with each other, even though this is the last time I'll ever see him alone. What's the point of moving on if you're not at peace with what's gone before it?

'I'm selling it,' he said. 'I need the money to go.'

'Do you not want to bring it with you then?' I said, thinking of that awful band he used to play with, thinking how that night when he was six must have crushed his will to succeed. And Corinne was just as bad. It was as if she thought, somewhere in the distortion of her buried consciousness, that if she was a major slut and shagged all those bands, she would never feel the pain of having it forced on her again, because she had done it willingly.

'No,' said Rob. 'I'm finished with all that. You should stick with the guitar though. You're the only one of us that was ever any good.'

'Will you come and see Corinne before you go?' I asked.

'Yes, he said. I wanted to ask him how he felt about Shane. And how he felt about Corinne forgetting what had happened in the past, burying it beneath the surface of her memory. But for some reason, I didn't. I had heard enough already, said enough today. So I just said goodbye forever, deeply sorry for him, full of regret for what might have been and hoping that somehow, somewhere, things would work out for him.

Twenty-nine

Rob rang two days later and arranged to meet Corinne in town, to say goodbye to her. When she came home, I could see that she'd been crying, but she said that she felt better for having seen him and said goodbye properly. She never told me exactly what had been said. That was between the two of them, and better left that way. But I did miss Rob, once I knew he was finally gone.

And what were we to do now? Corinne used to say that she felt better when she was away from here. Now we knew what it was about the landscape that troubled her so. We understood what it was that had kept driving her away, and what it was that had brought her home. Now, this place's hold on her was gone, and yet more days went by and we remained there, no longer oppressed by it, but unsettled and stifled by its implications. So it came as no surprise when Corinne suggested that we both leave together.

'We might as well,' she said. 'Make a fresh start of it.'

'Are you sure you're up to it yet?' I asked.

Ever since Shane's funeral, she had pretty much calmed down, but she seemed tired a lot of the time, and she still tended to brood a lot.

'Oh yeah,' she said. 'And it'd do me the world of good to get away.'

'That's what Rob said,' I reminded her. 'He said it was time to move on.'

'He's right,' she said. Corinne paused before adding, 'I know it's going to hurt a long time, and it's probably not over yet, but now that I know what happened to me, and now that I've faced up to it, at least I can start dealing with it, can't I?'

She was right. So I set the whole thing in motion without a second thought, driven from inside by some will to survive. The worst thing about it was telling Mam. We'd have to tell her everything, so that she'd understand. When we had done that, she sat in stunned, ineffectual shock, completely out of her depth.

'But, you, you can't just up and leave. You have to deal with this,' she told Corinne. 'Why don't you go back to the doctor that dealt with you before, and get some more counselling?'

'Counselling just made me feel worse before, when I didn't know what was wrong with me. And I don't see what difference it would make to me now that I do know. I'm just going to have to learn to live with it, and none of them people can tell me how to do that.'

'And what about you, Merle?' Mam said to me. 'I hope you're not just dropping out of college because you think you should be with your sister.'

'No Mam. I didn't want to go in the first place, and anyway, I was only there like about two days. I'm surprised they haven't written to kick me out yet.'

'But what are you going to do with yourself? At least Corinne has some kind of qualification.'

'I don't know, and I don't care. I'm going to bring my music with me, and that's the most important thing. I have that, and Corinne has nothing. Her so-called qualification means nothing to her.'

Mam asked Corinne what she wanted out of life. Corinne told

her that she honestly did not know but hoped to find out one day, and then the two of them cried. I didn't, I just sat there feeling relieved, so much pressure was lifting away.

Hannah cried when I told her that we were leaving. But she understood. She said she didn't know what she'd do without me, but I knew that she'd go back to college and get on with her life. It was different for her, she said. She had wanted to go to college, and she wasn't as worried for the future as she had been before, because she knew now that Shane's graphic deterioration during her childhood had not been his fault, and she had come to terms with him. So she was beginning to feel stronger now, for some reason.

And that was it, really. All that remained was for me and Corinne to pack our bags and go. We left one winter's morning, while the worn-out sun was struggling to shine a weak ray of light in the ice-blue sky.